Tipi

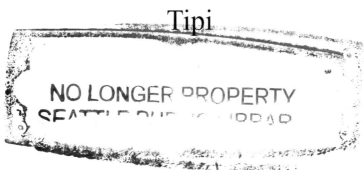

Tipi
Home of the Nomadic Buffalo Hunters

written and illustrated by
Paul Goble

Foreword by
Rodney Frey

World Wisdom

Tipi: Home of the Nomadic Buffalo Hunters
© World Wisdom, Inc. 2007

Pg. 44 [Sacred Otter steps inside tipi to meet Storm Maker, Bringer of Blizzards] drawing by Paul Goble, © 2000, Library of Congress, Prints and Photographs Division, gift of the artist (LC-DIG-ppmsca-02220)

Illustrations at the top of page 46, 67, 68, 72, 73, 76, 78, 99, 118, and at the bottom of pages 116, 117, and 119 were lent from the collection of Paul Goble artwork by the South Dakota Art Museum, Brookings, South Dakota.

Illustrations at the top of page 98, lent by Michael Fitzgerald

Library of Congress Cataloging-in-Publication Data

Goble, Paul.
  Tipi : home of the nomadic buffalo hunters / written and illustrated by Paul Goble ; foreword by Rodney Frey.
     p. cm.
  Includes bibliographical references and index.
  ISBN-13: 978-1-933316-37-6 (pbk. : alk. paper)
  ISBN-10: 1-933316-37-3 (pbk. : alk. paper)
  ISBN-13: 978-1-933316-39-0 (hardcover : alk. paper)
  ISBN-10: 1-933316-39-X (hardcover : alk. paper) 1. Tipis. 2. Indians of North America--Dwellings. I. Title.
  E98.D9.G63 2007
  728.089'97078--dc22

                                                              2006038705

Printed on acid-free paper in China
For information address World Wisdom, Inc.
P.O. Box 2682, Bloomington, Indiana 47402-2682
www.worldwisdom.com

Thank You
From time to time I have sought information about tipis from many people, whom I would like to thank: Kenny Harragarra for unpublished Kiowa and Kiowa-Apache designs; Nancy Fagin for color slides of Cheyenne designs in the Field Museum; Mike Cowdrey for a gold-mine of old photographs of Blackfoot tipis; Ted Brasser for Sarsi, Plains Cree, Assiniboin and Ojibwa designs; Winfield Coleman for help with Cheyenne and Arapaho tipi attachments. I also want to thank for their kind help: Larry Belitz, Dennis Carter, Peter Durkin, Rodney Frey, Neil Gilbert, Mark Hertig, Kevin Locke, Fr Peter Powell, Colin Taylor, and Ken Woody.

The mistakes in this book are mine. Thank you, my best beloved wife, Janet. It has been a delight to work on this book, and on every other one of the books, together. I have been constantly seeking your opinion on the writing and matters of aesthetics. The work has been all joy. Thank you. Paul.

Author's Note

My experience with tipis is quite humble, as the omissions and mistakes in this book will show. When living in the Black Hills, I cut and peeled a set of poles, and had a tipi for a few years, but I have always been more interested in drawing and painting them. I have never had the good fortune to paint a tipi cover, nor to watch one painted.

I have helped Indian people pitch and strike tipis, and I have lived in them during summer gatherings. My first experiences were at the 1959 Rodeo in Sheridan, Wyoming, and at the American Indian Days, when Tom and Suzie Yellowtail of the Crow Nation gave me the use of one of their tipis, a Cheyenne tipi with attached beadwork decorations, illustrated on page 97. Pitched close by was the red and yellow striped tipi of Alba and Hattie Shawaway of the Yakima Nation, illustrated on page 107.

Another early experience was in the company of several Crow Indian families, when Reginald and Gladys Laubin generously lent us their tipis for the night. It was unforgettable to actually sleep in their red top tipi, complete with its beautiful furnishings, as shown in their book, *The Indian Tipi—Its History, Construction, and Use*, published in 1957 by the University of Oklahoma.

It was never my intention to write a book about tipis. The Laubins had already written the definitive book. It was just that I liked to collect examples of painted tipis, and to try to draw them. Over the years a pile of drawings grew. I always hoped that someone who was writing about tipis might have been able to use some of the illustrations. With this in mind I sent the artwork, first to the University of Nebraska Press, where it remained for some years, and then to the University of Oklahoma Press, but without success. Rather than the paintings should remain unused, I have tried to make the book myself. Everyone who wants to know more must consult the Laubins' book, as indeed I have done, holding their book in my left hand while working with my right.

Many of these illustrations were drawn over twenty years ago, which has resulted in different drawing styles, and levels of competence. The designs are carefully copied, with tracings, photo enlargements or reductions. Photographs might have been preferred, but museums guard their photographs with reproduction fees, making it impossible to present many designs in one book. Some of these designs date from nomadic Buffalo Days. I have only included more recent designs which I feel fit comfortably within the tribal traditions; another book would be needed to illustrate the numerous modern designs. It is impossible to speculate on the color in old black- and-white photographs, but where I have done so, it is noted in the texts, and I have avoided illustrating designs which are only partially visible, or of those too indistinct to be certain.

In this work, I have always been conscious that I am painting people's most personal dreams. It has been done out of admiration, wishing not to offend the spirits of the original owners of the tipis, their present-day descendants, nor the blessed bird or animal spirits, who gave these designs to people in dreams.

A Note for Teachers and Librarians

Over the years you have sent me many photographs and letters about projects which you have carried out with your students on aspects of Native American culture. You have forwarded your students' letters and paintings, which I have faithfully answered! Time and again I have noticed your need of help with tipis, their construction, and above all their painted designs. Here there are design ideas galore, which I hope will be helpful, and pages to photocopy for students to cut and color model tipis.

A Special Note for Young Readers

When I was your age my mother made me a small tipi and painted it with Native American symbols. It excited my interest, and made me want to know more. This book is the kind of book I began looking for, but never found. So I have made it for you. I hope you enjoy it, like I have loved the thrill of discovering all these stories and gloriously colored tipis.

Foreword

Each semester a new group of my students gather under a clear sky on a grassy field somewhere on campus. They are presented with some wood and fiber, specifically, sixteen poles of lodgepole pine, peeled clean; a set of sharpened chokecherry-wood stakes and willow pins; some twenty feet of hemp rope; and a large section of canvas, cut and sown into a half-circle and painted with strips, dots, and animal images. And they are given the task of raising a tipi.

There is an immediate wonder in their eyes, along with a bit of apprehension. Where do we start? How do we tie the poles together and set them up? How do we get the cover over the poles? What is the meaning of these painted images? Why is the lodge to face east? And the questions continue.

After a few helpful hints and typically a false start or two, the tipi is raised. All the students are then invited to enter. With amazement from each, all twenty plus students comfortably fit into the rather small, twelve-foot lodge. With the burning of tobacco from a cigarette, a prayer of thanks is offered. As the smoke ascends through the smoke flaps, so too do the words. It is a prayer to the Lodge, renewing its vitality and asking that all who have entered it be blessed and kept safe, and that the teachings of the Lodge continue for all to appreciate.

The raised tipi is known as the Otter Lodge, a gift presented in 1982 to all my students, both present and future, from George and Molly Kicking Woman of Browning, Montana. The Lodge has long belonged to the Kicking Woman family, handed down within the family from generation to generation. As with other painted lodges, this lodge was a gift from the Spirit Animal People, in this case, the Otter, with the cover of images and colors telling its story and offering its protection.

With their newly acquired skills, effort, and much heart, the students have transformed the pieces of wood and fiber into a home. It is a home that in a Montana gale, will hug the earth all the tighter. Under a clear sky, it allows the light of the moon and stars to fill its interior. During the summer's heat, it welcomes a cooling breeze under its rolled-up cover. During the winter's cold, with even a smallest fire, the lodge keeps its inhabitants warm and cozy. With its silhouette atop a hill, against a tree line, beside a stream, or amongst a camp of other tipis, the Lodge stands in perfect harmony with its environment. The pieces of wood and fiber have been transformed into the Lodge, a Lodge with its own personality and volition, with its power to watch over and protect its inhabitants.

I have had the pleasure of knowing Paul for almost thirty years, and in the pages of each new story book he has brought forth during those years I have beheld a new excitement, wonder, and beauty. That excitement and beauty most certainly continues here. As the experience of raising a tipi has done for my students, Paul's *Tipi: Home of the Nomadic Buffalo Hunters* opens the door of the Lodge for all to enter its interior. The history and culture, the architecture and aesthetics, the very heart of the tipi are revealed and experienced in its true spirit and splendor. Paul is particularly sensitive to the spiritual dimensions of the tipi, telling of the prayers to and the stories of the guardian spirit birds and animals with respect and honor. Any questions you may bring to the raising of the tipi are, in the pages ahead, given answers with clarity, authenticity, accuracy, and the eye of a true artist. So now enter and experience for yourself the pieces of wood and fiber transformed into the wondrous *Tipi*.

Rodney Frey
University of Idaho

6

IN THE VERY BEGINNING, when the Creator had made First Man and First Woman, he told his Helper in the work of Creation: "Stay close to Man and Woman, and look after all their needs."

When the first winds of winter blew, Man and Woman shivered, huddling close to their cooking fire.

The Creator's Helper knew they would need a shelter. Tradition tells that it was the shape of the leaf of the rustling Cottonwood tree which gave him the idea.

The materials which the Creator's Helper chose for Man and Woman's shelter were straight and slender trunks of Pine trees for *poles*; strong Ash wood branches for *pegs*; thin Chokecherry shoots for *pins*; tanned Buffalo Cow skins for the *cover*; Buffalo Bull raw-hide for *rope*; and a tanned Buffalo Calf skin for the *door*.

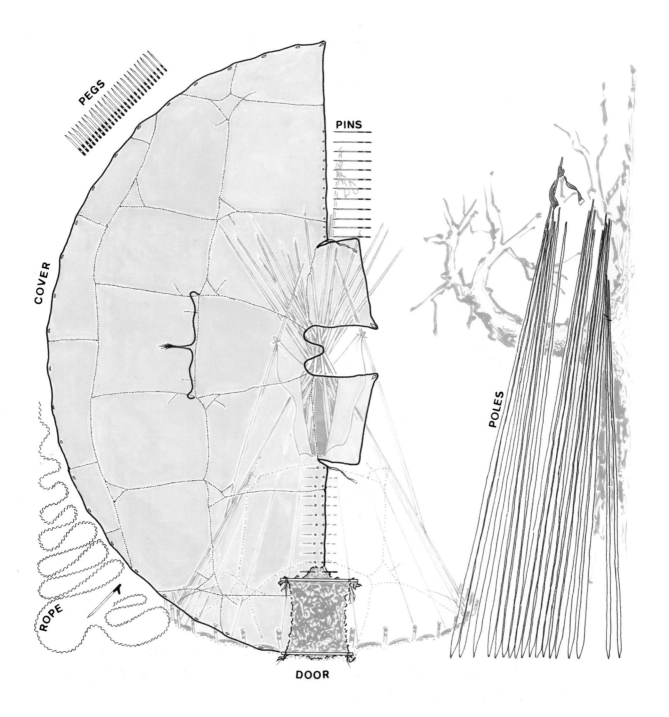

PEGS

PINS

COVER

POLES

ROPE

DOOR

The shelter is known by many names. Webster's dictionary calls it "*teepee* or *tipi*, Dakota from *ti* to dwell, and *pi* used for." The Lakota use *tipi*, but the older word is *tipestola*, "she or he lives in a sharp pointed lodge." Blackfoot people call it *niitoyis*; the Kiowa, *do-heen*.

The Creator's Helper made the *tipi* a beautiful home, with a cover upon which people would paint their dreams, and a smoke hole so they could look up at the Above World.

Tipi Doors Face East
The tipi of First Man and First Woman
was pitched with its door to the East.
Each day they woke to see Morning Star rising,
and were greeted by Sun's first yellow rays
shining through the smoke hole and the door,
filling their lodge with holy light.
The descendants of First Man and First Woman pitch
their tipis in a circle, and each tipi faces the East,
except at the time of the annual Sun Dance
when the tipis face the center.
Every circle of tipis has a doorway
toward the East.
So it was, and always will be.

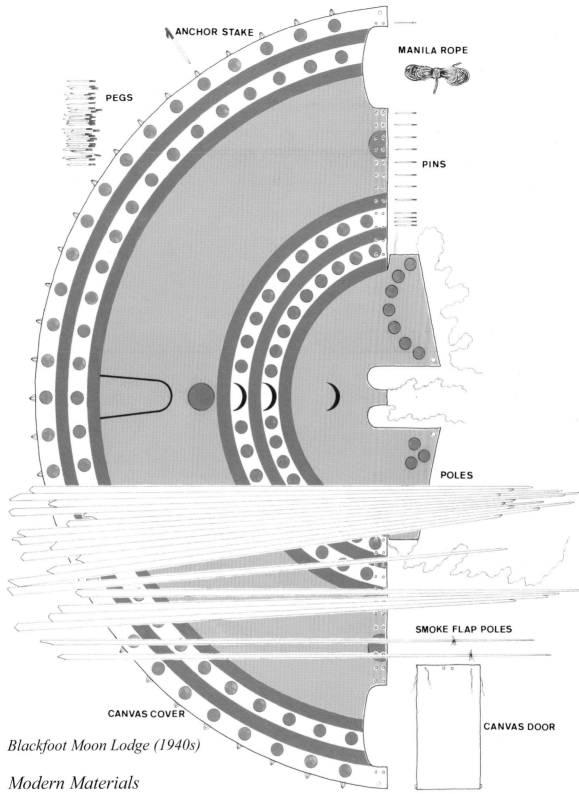

ANCHOR STAKE

MANILA ROPE

PEGS

PINS

POLES

SMOKE FLAP POLES

CANVAS COVER

CANVAS DOOR

Blackfoot Moon Lodge (1940s)

Modern Materials

The structure of the tipi has not changed since the old days, but some of the materials are different: cotton duck canvas replaced buffalo hides for the cover and door during the 1880s; cotton cord and hemp rope, instead of rawhide; synthetic threads replace sinew for stitching; and commercial house paints are used instead of natural pigments.

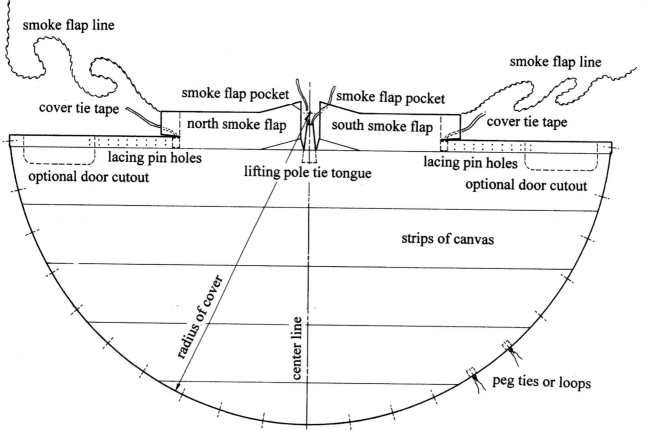

smoke flap line

smoke flap line

smoke flap pocket   smoke flap pocket

cover tie tape

north smoke flap   south smoke flap   cover tie tape

lacing pin holes   lacing pin holes

optional door cutout   optional door cutout

lifting pole tie tongue

strips of canvas

radius of cover

center line

peg ties or loops

Cover

For a tipi cover, men killed the needed buffalo in the springtime. The number of hides required depended on how many were to live in the tipi, and on the available horses to transport it. Always an even number, 16 to 20 hides were needed for most tipis. People honored the buffalo that they gave their lives so people could be sheltered, clothed, and fed. It had been thus ordained in the beginning times.

When the women had finished the heavy work of tanning the hides, many women gathered on an appointed day to sew the cover, led by one who was experienced. The day started early with prayer, and as they worked with bone awls and sinew thread, each kept happy thoughts in her mind, so that all who lived in the tipi would be happy. The cover was finished within the day.

The tipi was pitched, the smoke flaps and door tightly shut, and a fire of sagebrush burned inside. The cover was smoked to a pale yellow ochre so it would not become hard after a rain. A tipi with a smoked cover was translucent and bright inside. If there were paintings on the outside, they showed through on the inside like murals.

After white hunters slaughtered the buffalo herds in the 1880s, covers were made of canvas. The material being easier to work and lighter to transport, tipis tended to be larger, but the design did not change.

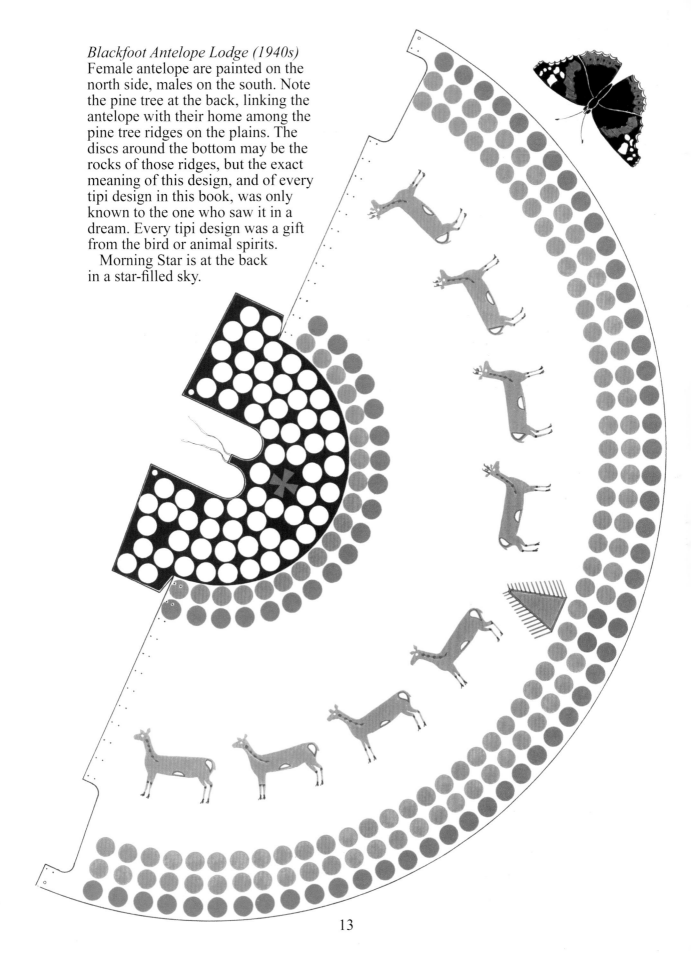

Blackfoot Antelope Lodge (1940s)
Female antelope are painted on the north side, males on the south. Note the pine tree at the back, linking the antelope with their home among the pine tree ridges on the plains. The discs around the bottom may be the rocks of those ridges, but the exact meaning of this design, and of every tipi design in this book, was only known to the one who saw it in a dream. Every tipi design was a gift from the bird or animal spirits.

Morning Star is at the back in a star-filled sky.

13

Poles

Lodgepole Pine, as the name suggests, makes the ideal tipi pole, although any other straight, stiff, and slim tree will do. Young trees that have grown up close together, struggling for the light, are the best because they are straight and almost without branches. It is easiest to peel pine bark in the spring when the sap is flowing. This leaves the poles smooth and almost polished when they are dry. Any remaining rough spots from twig stems then need to be smoothed to prevent wear on the cover, and to allow rain to run down the poles.

The length depends on the size of the tipi. Twenty-five feet poles should be about 4 inches at the butts, and 2 inches where they meet. The butts need to be axed to a point.

On the treeless plains it could mean a long journey every few years to the closest pine forest to replace tipi poles. Men helped with the heavy work of cutting and peeling. A set of eighteen poles represented a considerable amount of work and was reckoned to be worth two good horses. The worst punishment that camp police very occasionally meted out was to break a family's tipi poles.

14

Drying Tipi Poles

You will know when you are in Indian Country because you will see tipi poles resting comfortably in the crotch of shade trees. In the drawing, a set of newly cut poles has been stacked into a narrow pyramid to prevent them getting a permanent bow. They will need to be turned often while they dry over several weeks. Here the decorative topmost needles have been left, which would never have been done during Buffalo Days, and before summer's end the needles will have turned brown and brittle.

Pole Lengths Vary

The length that tipi poles project above the tipi is a matter of choice. In Buffalo Days poles were dragged by horses from one campsite to another, resulting in much wear and rough usage, which kept the poles relatively short. These days poles receive only part-time use and are elegant by comparison, lighter and more fragile, and often of exaggerated lengths projecting far above the tipi.

In the early reservation days, the 1880s, there was a Lakota Red Top Tipi Society. It was an old warriors' society whose members met in a tipi with a red top. They no doubt reminisced about their warrior days when they were young, raiding the Crow and Pawnee horse herds.

SARSI

PLAINS CREE

BLACKFOOT

PLAINS OJIBWA

KUTENAI
YAKIMA

GROS VENTRE

ASSINIBOIN

HIDATSA
MANDAN
ARIKARA

FLATHEAD

CROW

NEZ PERCE

TETON SIOUX

PONCA

EASTERN SIOUX

SHOSHONI

CHEYENNE

OMAHA

ARAPAHO

PAWNEE

OTO

UTE

CHEYENNE

KIOWA

COMANCHE

WICHITA

▲△ THREE-POLE   ■ □ FOUR-POLE BASE TIPIS

▲ ■ NOMADIC   △ □ SEMI-NOMADIC

Three-Pole and Four-Pole Peoples

16

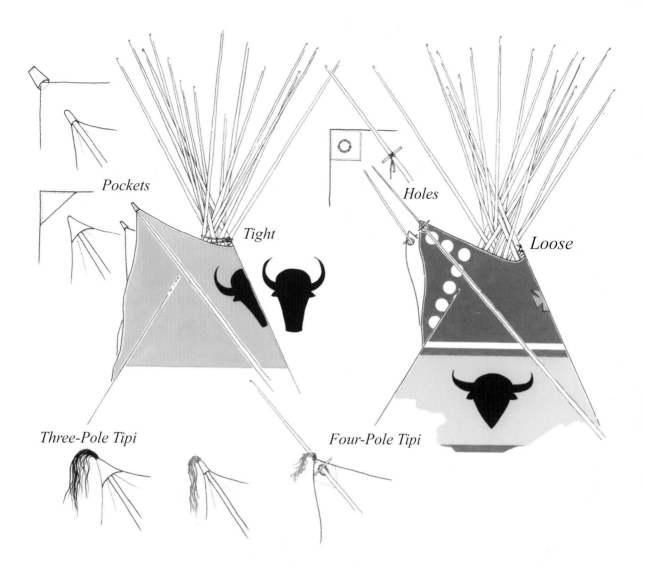

Pockets

Tight

Holes

Loose

Three-Pole Tipi

Four-Pole Tipi

Telling Three- and Four-Pole Base Tipis Apart

There are three-pole and four-pole peoples, meaning those who use either three or four poles for the foundation of their tipis, a triangular or square base. At first glance all tipis might look alike, but the smoke flaps are different. It is a matter of *pockets* or *holes*: on three-pole tipis the smoke flap poles poke into *pockets*; on four-pole tipis the smoke flap poles pass through *holes*.

The three-pole tipi cone is tilted; the four-pole is less so, and the cone looks squatter. Three-pole tipis cross their poles in a *tight* cluster; four-poles in a *loose* bunch.

Four-pole tipis tend to need exterior guy ropes to prevent them blowing down in a wind; the three-pole structure is sturdier because of its tripod base and the anchor rope which is tightened around the poles where they meet. It is also sturdier because most of the poles are placed in the front (east) crotch, bracing against the prevailing (west) wind.

Pegs and Anchor Stakes

Pegs are best cut from young ash trees, but any tough wood is good, about 1 inch diameter and 18 inches long, axed to a sharp point. Anchor stakes about 1 3/4 inches diameter, and 2 feet long, and pointed. Several inches of bark are left on the blunt end, helping to stop the peg strings or loops from slipping. Pegs with branch stumps, as illustrated, are another way to help this, but rather than cut down a forest searching for them, straight pegs are the norm, driven in slightly angled out from the lodge cover. The bark is often carved into decorative rings, and sometimes rubbed with powdered paint.

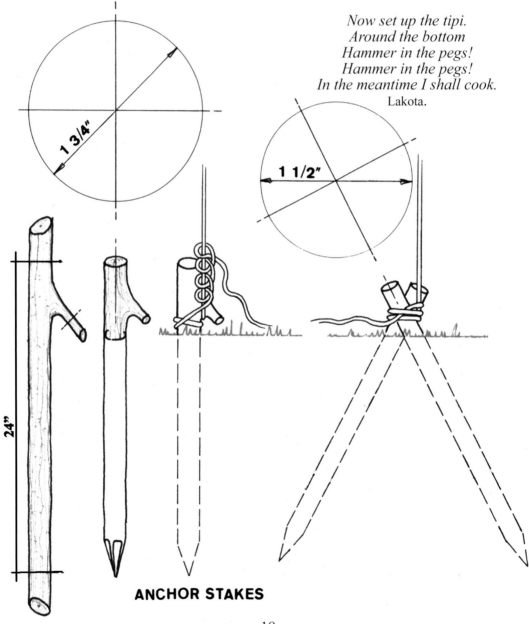

*Now set up the tipi.
Around the bottom
Hammer in the pegs!
Hammer in the pegs!
In the meantime I shall cook.*
Lakota.

ANCHOR STAKES

18

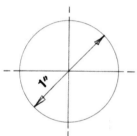

Blackfoot Lodge (1950s)

This lodge has an exterior anchor. Occasionally two exterior anchors are used, mostly with four-pole base tipis which stand less wind than three-pole tipis. With an exterior anchor, and with the pointed tipi poles poked well into the ground, any tipi should stand high winds.

Note the tidy oval flap door, and the flags at the tips of the smoke flap poles. Besides the uncertain animal design—is it a wolf?—the really strange thing about this tipi is that the smoke flaps are painted on both the outside, *and inside.* During Buffalo Days the inside of the smoke flaps quickly became black with soot from the cooking fires, as did the whole top of the tipi.

The regulation of the smoke draft was an old excuse for young unmarried women to go outside after dark to meet their sweethearts. If a girl knew that her lover was near her lodge, she would say, "It seems so smoky in here, perhaps the wind has changed. I must go out to adjust the flaps."
Assiniboin.

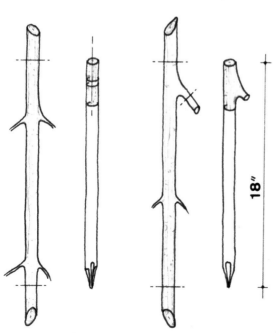

PEGS

19

Lacing Pins

These join the tipi cover at the front. Each is about 3/8th inch diameter and 14 inches long, and like arrows, are best made from straight young chokecherry shoots. Once the bark is removed, but leaving decorative rings at one end, and the pins cut to length, they are tied into a bundle to keep them straight while the wood dries. They are then ready to be smoothed and sharpened at one end.

Ceremonial Lodge

For some sacred ceremonies which had to be conducted away from the general view, two tipis were temporarily pitched against each other. The covers were unpinned at the front, and the structure strengthened with exterior anchor ropes.

Opposite: a Blackfoot Striped Lodge and a Buffalo Track Lodge (1950s) have been joined.

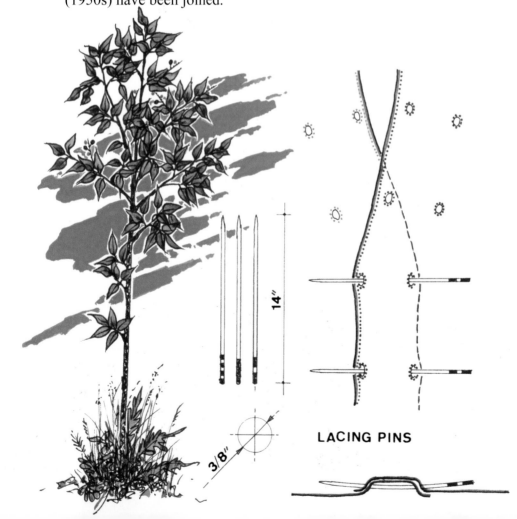

14"

3/8"

LACING PINS

Pinning the Cover

These ladies have improvised a way to reach the topmost lacing pins. Usually the pins that are out of reach are fastened by a boy or girl who climbs up the lower pins, as can be seen in the Indian drawing, opposite. When the women have pinned the cover, they will go inside and push the poles outward to tighten the cover.

This is the Blackfoot All Star Lodge (1940s). In the story of the lodge's origin it is told that a man had failed for many days to find the buffalo, and his family were hungry. He told his wife: "If I do not find any buffalo today, I will sleep out in the hills until I can bring you and the children something to eat."

That night he dreamed a man took him to his tipi and said: "My son, you are already among the buffalo, but you cannot see them! I feel sorry for you. The stars you see painted all over my lodge are not stars at all; they are buffalo dung. Copy my lodge, and you will never be hungry, because you will always be right among the buffalo herds."

Figure 1

Figure 2

Doors
The tipi may look beautifully pitched and magnificently painted, but the door can often look a bit of an afterthought, improvised with various materials and colors. Doors are hung from one of the lower lacing pins, and attached with additional tapes or pins through the cover. Because it rains little on the Great Plains, a truly watertight door is not a priority.

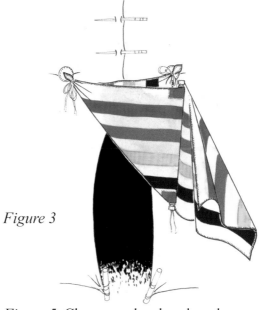

Figure 3

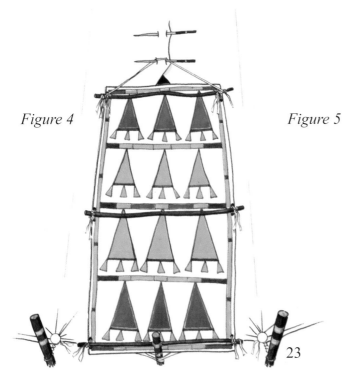

Figure 4

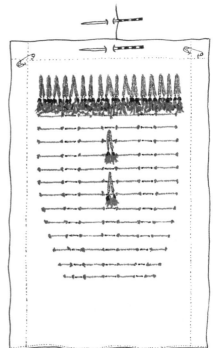

Figure 5

Figure 1. Crow: a canvas door hung from a lacing pin. Note the pins!
Figure 2. Various canvas doors: some with stick frames, others that roll up.
Figure 3. Cloth or blanket with a stick to keep it spread is the most common type of door. To open, the stick is twisted to one side and dropped on the sloping tipi cover. In the old days doors were mostly either tanned buffalo hide like the cover, or an animal skin, hair side out to help shed rain.
Figure 4. Crow: old painted rawhide, beautiful, but heavy, and needing three stick spreaders to keep it flat.

Figure 5. Cheyenne: beadwork and tassels on canvas.

A closed tipi door is "locked." Visitors need only cough or tap the cover to announce themselves. Formerly there was no thieving within a community. George Catlin, the Indian painter, writing in the 1830s: *"I have roamed about during seven or eight years, visiting and associating with some three or four hundred thousand of these people. No Indian ever betrayed me, struck me a blow, or stole a shilling's worth of my property that I am aware of."*

23

It is Difficult to Poke the Poles Through the Smoke Flap Holes

When holding a long, heavy, and wobbly smoke flap pole, it is not easy to get the tip of it through the hole in the smoke flap. There is a story that tells how Blackfoot women were helped in this:

Once, when picking berries, a woman came across a burial place where a body had been placed on a platform in the fork of a tree. The bones had fallen through and were scattered around beneath. She carefully gathered them up and put them back. As she did this, she said: "I do not know who you are, or when you died, but I will put you back again. And, yes, I will bring you food as well."

She did this from time to time. One day she fell asleep under the tree, and while sleeping a girl came to her and said: "Sister, you have been kind to me. I will help you with your work." After that, whenever the woman was tired, tanning hides or gathering firewood, she called upon the Spirit Girl to help, and her work was made easy.

One night when it was snowing a pole came out of the hole in the smoke flap. She poked around with the pole to put it back, but in the dark she could not find the hole. She called upon the Spirit Girl to help her, and at once the pole went through the hole.

It became the custom that whenever women were trying to poke the poles through the smoke flap holes, they would ask the Spirit Girl for help.

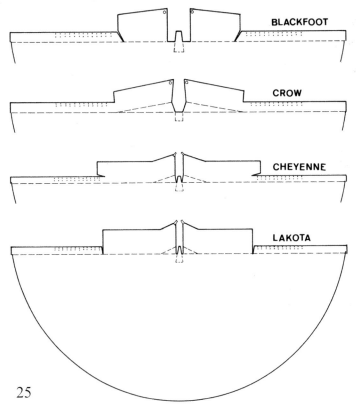

Shapes of Smoke Flaps
The preferred shapes of smoke flaps varies a little from one people to another, although differences are blurred. The Cheyenne prefer long narrow flaps, the Lakota shorter and wider. The shapes to the right are approximations. Note the wide gap between the Blackfoot flaps, to accommodate the loose four-pole stack, compared with the small gap for tight three-pole Cheyenne and Lakota stacks.

Also note that whereas a door cut-out is usual today, no cut-out used to be common. When the tipi is pitched, the cover, between the bottom lacing pin and the peg loops on the ground, falls naturally into a narrow oval opening, sufficient for a doorway.

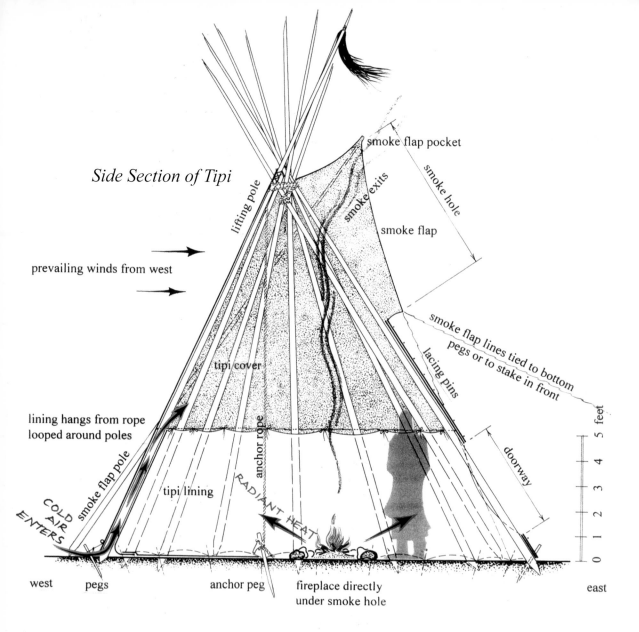

Side Section of Tipi

smoke flap pocket

smoke hole

smoke flap

lifting pole

smoke exits

prevailing winds from west

smoke flap lines tied to bottom pegs or to stake in front

tipi cover

lacing pins

lining hangs from rope looped around poles

anchor rope

doorway

5 feet

smoke flap pole

RADIANT HEAT

tipi lining

4

3

COLD AIR ENTERS

2

1

0

west   pegs   anchor peg   fireplace directly   east
                                                  under smoke hole

Heating and Ventilating the Tipi

A small fire gives comfortable radiant heat, and as the hot air rises, much is trapped by the smaller top of the tipi's cone, giving all-round warmth.

The smoke flaps act like a coat collar, keeping the wind from blowing down into the tipi and filling it with smoke. By directing the flaps, smoke is drawn out of the lodge. The smoke hole, being to some extent sheltered on the leeward side of the tipi and so not in the center, allows the fireplace to be closer to the door (see ground plan opposite). This gives more living room at the back of the lodge, and because of the steeper angle of the poles at the back, there is more headroom. Areas close to the edge under the cover are for storage and sleeping.

The tipi is much better to live in; always clean, warm in winter, cool in summer; easy to move. The white man builds big house, cost much money, like big cage, shut out sun, can never move; always sick.
Flying Hawk, Lakota.

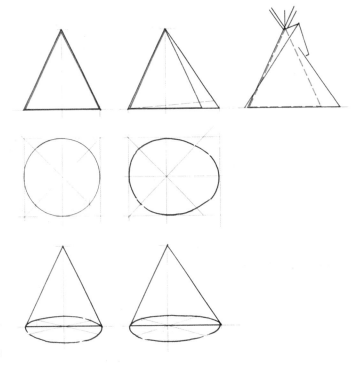

The Tipi is a Tilted Cone

The tipi's shape is not a true cone, being steeper at the back, the west, (remembering that the tipi faces east). Most of the poles are at the east, bracing against the pressure of the prevailing winds from the west and northwest, blowing against the steep west side. Without any corners, a cone easily sheds wind and rain.

Since the tipi is not a true cone, the floor plan is not round but shaped a little like an egg, longer from the door to the back, east to west.

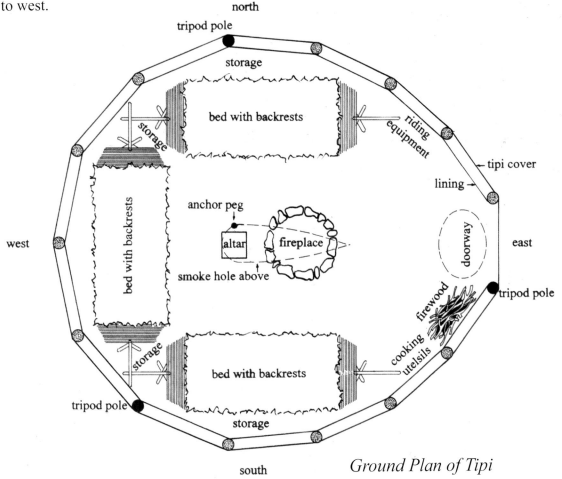

Ground Plan of Tipi

27

Setting-up a Three-Pole Base Tipi

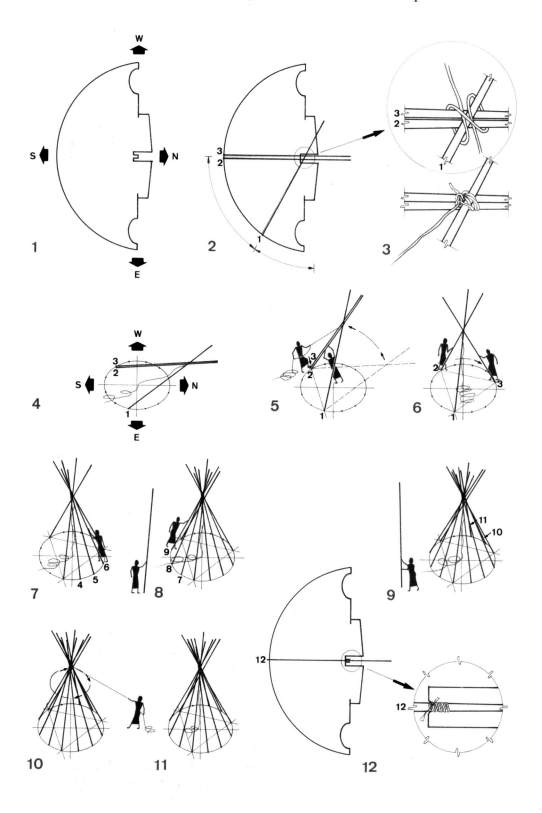

28

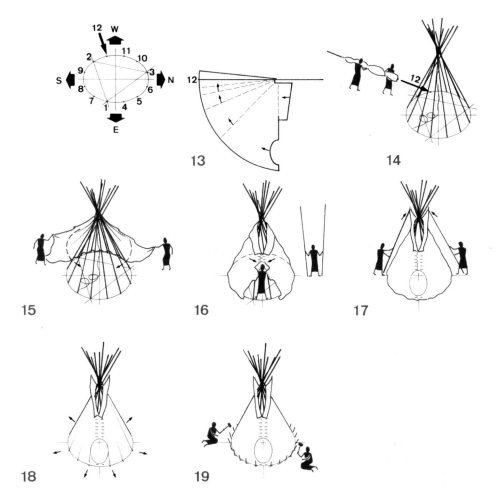

1. Lay tipi cover on the ground with straight side on an east/west axis.

2. Place two poles on a north/south axis, with their butts projecting slightly from the edge of the cover. Place another pole about 2/3 the distance between south and east.

3. With one end of a long rope, tie a clove hitch where the poles cross. Wrap rope around and finish with another clove hitch or square knot.

4. Keeping poles in the same alignment, lift them off the cover and place where tipi is to be pitched.

5. Raise the three poles by pulling on the rope.

6. Leave poles #1 and #2 in place. Spread pole #3, tightening the knot, forming a tripod foundation.

7. Place poles #4, #5, and #6 into crotch of tripod.

8. Place poles #7, #8, and #9 into the opposite crotch

9. Place poles #10 and #11.

10. Take rope three times tightly around the poles where they all meet.

11. All poles are now in place, except #12, called the lifting pole.

12. Lay the lifting pole on the cover. Secure the tie tongue to the pole.

13. Fold the cover against the pole.

14. Two people are needed to lift the heavy cover and pole. Place butt at west. Raise into the crotch.

15. Pull the cover around the poles.

16. Join the cover at the front with lacing pins.

17. Poke tips of slender poles into pockets on smoke flaps.

18. From inside, push poles outward to tighten cover.

19. Hammer in pegs around bottom. Hammer in anchor peg where rope hangs from crotch, and tie.

29

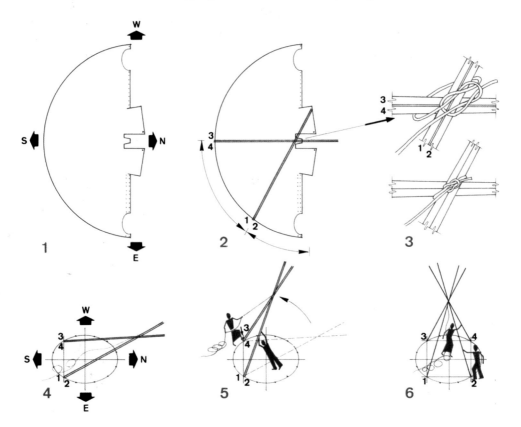

1. Lay cover on ground with straight side on an east/west axis.

2. Place two poles on a north/south axis with butts projecting slightly from edge of cover. Place two more poles about 2/3 distance between south and east.

3. With one end of a long rope, tie a square knot where poles meet. Wrap tightly and tie.

4. Keeping poles in same alignment, place where tipi is to be pitched.

5. Raise poles by pulling on rope.

6. Leave poles #1 and #3 in place. Spread #2 and #4, tightening knot and forming a square base.

7. Place poles #5 and #6 in crotch.

8. Place poles #7 and #8 in crotch.

9. Place pole #9.

10. Place poles #10 and #11 either side of door.

11. Eleven poles now in place.

12. #12 Lifting pole.

13. Lay lifting pole on cover. Secure tie tongue to pole.

14. Fold cover against pole.

15. Two people are needed to lift cover and pole. Place butt at west, and raise into crotch.

16. Pull cover around poles.

17. Join cover with lacing pins.

18. Poke end of smoke flap poles through smoke flaps.

19. From inside, push poles outward to tighten cover.

20. Hammer in pegs around bottom.

21. Hammer in anchor stake where rope hangs down, and tie.

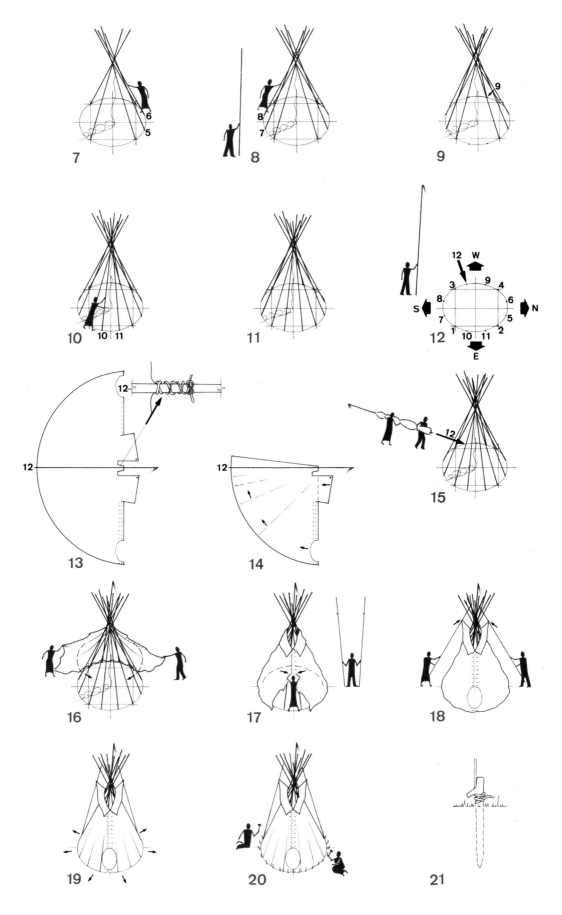

Tipis Belonged to the Women

Whether painted according to the man's dream, or unpainted, the tipi was the property of the woman. Although men often helped to cut the poles, women peeled them and ensured they were smooth and would not wear holes in the cover. A little above where the poles crossed, she burned holes through each pole to tie them to the pack saddle. She knew which were her sturdy foundation poles, and which her lifting pole. She made the cover, the lining, cut the pegs and pins, and made backrests and storage bags.

It was the women who chose where to camp, and each selected the site for her tipi, one which was level, free of gopher or snake holes, and well drained in case of a sudden storm. The women put up the tipis, and took them down, and packed everything on their horses.

Divorce was rare in Buffalo Days, but in theory the woman only had to throw the man's things outside the lodge. There was division of labor, men being the hunters and warriors. Today men help cutting and peeling the poles, but women are still in charge. The author has seen men holding tipi poles, waiting for the women to tell them in which crotch to place them. Women took, and still take, great pride in a well pitched and beautifully furnished lodge.

A beautiful tipi is like a good mother: she hugs her children and protects them from heat and cold, snow and rain.
Lakota saying.

Moving Camp

A family of six needed five pack horses to move camp: two or three horses dragged the tipi poles, heavy ends dragging. Extra load, even children atop, was carried on platforms fixed to the bunches of poles behind the horses, similar to travois poles. The tipi cover was the main load for a pack horse. Families with more horses could live in larger tipis and travel in greater comfort. Mules were stronger and could carry more. Men, as guardians, rode their fastest horses unencumbered.

Backrests

The Blackfoot favor taller backrests than the Cheyenne and Lakota (illustrated here). Depending upon the desired height, anywhere from 130 and 190 sandbar willows, peeled and straightened with the teeth, and often painted, are strung into a mat. This is hung against two of the poles of a tripod of ash poles, usually carved and painted, and having pointed ends which are pushed into the ground to give the backrest stability. Backrests are light and rolled for transport.

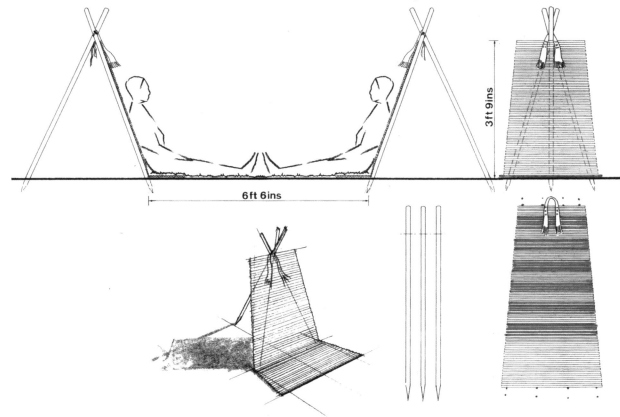

6ft 6ins

3ft 9ins

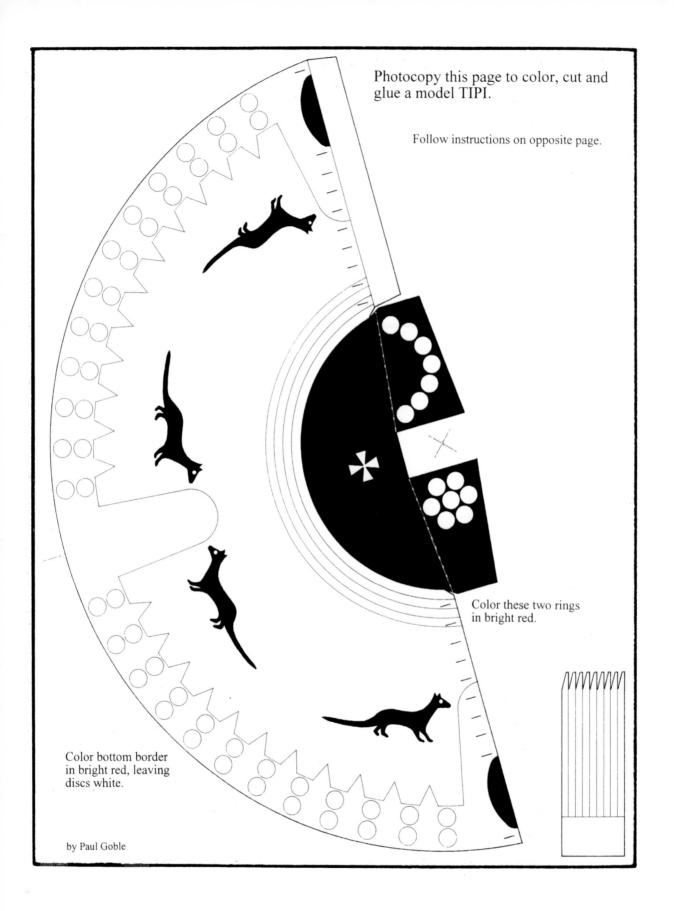

Photocopy this page to color, cut and glue a model TIPI.

Follow instructions on opposite page.

Color these two rings in bright red.

Color bottom border in bright red, leaving discs white.

by Paul Goble

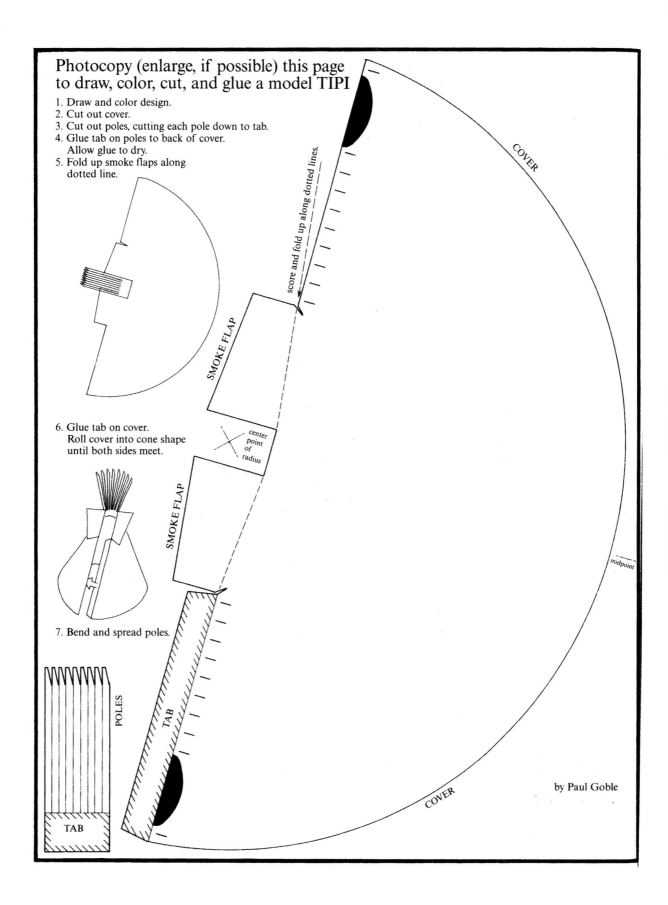

Photocopy (enlarge, if possible) this page to draw, color, cut, and glue a model TIPI

1. Draw and color design.
2. Cut out cover.
3. Cut out poles, cutting each pole down to tab.
4. Glue tab on poles to back of cover. Allow glue to dry.
5. Fold up smoke flaps along dotted line.

6. Glue tab on cover. Roll cover into cone shape until both sides meet.

7. Bend and spread poles.

score and fold up along dotted lines.

SMOKE FLAP

SMOKE FLAP

COVER

COVER

center point of radius

midpoint

POLES

TAB

TAB

by Paul Goble

Tipi Lining

The canvas tipi lining, formerly buffalo skins, is tied in sections to a rope which is looped around each of the poles at a little below shoulder height, starting at one doorway pole and ending at the other. Around the bottom, the lining is tucked under the floor covering, or rests upon it, and is held down either with logs, but usually with parfleche storage bags (see page 48).

Air is drawn under the bottom of the tipi cover, travels up between the cover and the lining, and because of the tipi's cone shape, the draft helps exit the smoke from the lodge.

38   Inside of tipi, looking up.

Beverly Hungry Wolf, Blood Indian from Alberta, told how she remembered her grandmother hanging the lining in her tipi:

After my grandmother got the outside of her tipi set up she went inside to put up her liner. That's the long curtain that hangs around inside and keeps the winds from blowing through. She tied her long lining cord to the main pole, the one at the back that held the cover. From there she brought the cord toward the doorway from both sides. She'd make a loop around every second pole with it, and she'd tie each end to the poles on each side of the doorway.

She'd take out her best tipi lining and she'd put it across where the main bed was going to be—her and my grandfather's bed. Then she'd put up the rest of her linings, right to the doorway. Then she'd put her parfleches around the inside of the tipi to hold down the bottoms of the liners, because they are heavily loaded with dried meat and pemmican.

Inside the Blackfoot Black Buffalo Lodge

Inside a painted tipi, a person feels surrounded by the protective presence of the spirit animals painted on the outside. The poles cross these shadow-like silhouettes, reaching out through the smoke hole to the zenith.

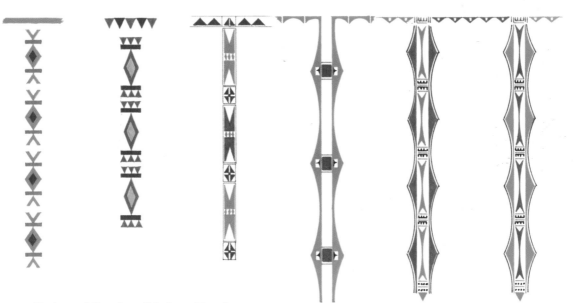

Painted Lodge Lining Designs

The designs on these pages usually have a relatively thin top horizontal border line or pattern. The wider vertical patterned stripes echo the lodge poles, but are not intended to match their spacing. Designs with more curvature may be Lakota or Cheyenne; the Blackfoot tend to favor more angular designs. Instead of geometric designs, which were painted by women, men sometimes painted the tipi's lining with their war and horse-raiding experiences.

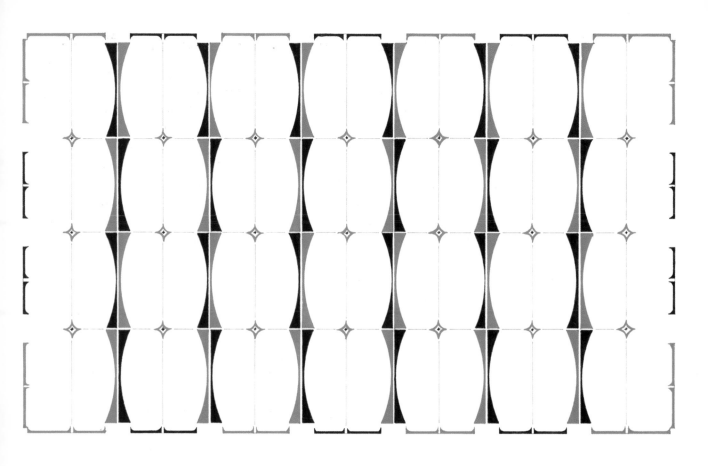

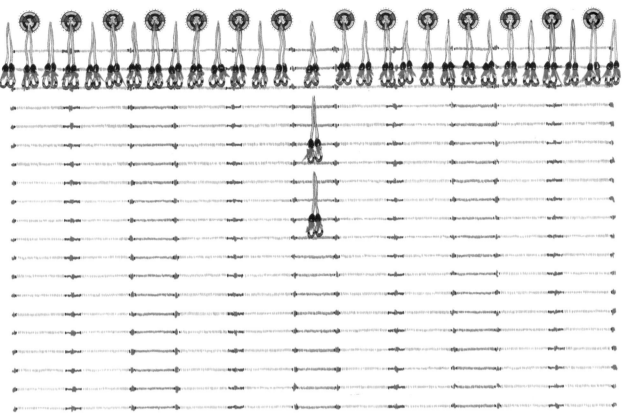

Lodge Linings, Dew Cloths
Above left, is an old Lakota design painted on tanned buffalo hide. All the lines are parallel, vertical or horizontal, but have you noticed that the design has the strange power to bend the lines and make your eyes go wibbly-wobbly?

Opposite, three Blackfoot lining designs.

Above, is a traditional Cheyenne single lining section, measuring about 8 feet wide, made by women of the Cheyenne Quill Workers Society. Formerly the design was worked in dyed porcupine quills on tanned buffalo hides, later with glass beads on canvas. The form is always 14 beaded discs, which is twice the sacred number 7 (west, north, east, south, sky, earth, and center). Each quill-wrapped tassel ends in a loop with a deer's dew claw, and red yarn (formerly buffalo hair). The colors were always red, yellow, black and white, although pale blue is now, often used instead of white.

In the Lakota drawing (1870s), below, the tipi has a painted earth base and sky top, with sacred rainbow circles either side. Note the serrated smoke flap edges and colored finials.

While the children play, the mother cleans a hide with an elk horn scraper. The meat hangs on a pole out of the reach of dogs to sun dry.

Painted Tipis

People sought, and still seek, throughout their lives to meet in a dream some spirit bird or animal that would give them guidance and protection during their lives. These were intermediaries between man and God, similar to patron saints and guardian angels, and therefore Indian people were not nature worshipers, as some have thought. A long tradition for the lonely vigil, fasting and praying on the hilltop, meant that the sought-after dreams did indeed come.

When a man received a dream about a tipi, he did not blurt it out to the first person he met, nor rush off and paint a cover. Ceremonies and prayers were first offered, and then the dreamer recounted his dream to the priests and wise men of the community, and it was discussed amongst them as to its meanings for the dreamer. Those known to be skilled painters were consulted, and the new design was made to fit anonymously within the traditional framework of their painted tipis. Neither originality of idea, nor individualistic styles of painting were sought. This is why Blackfoot, Kiowa, and Cheyenne tipis have their own tribal similarities and elements in common. Apart from some tipis painted with personal war and hunting experiences, nobody merely decorated a tipi to make it look pretty. All tipi painting sprung from a spiritual source.

Guardian Spirit Birds and Animals

The spirit bird or animal, or other object or force in nature, which gave the tipi design told the dreamer to make or gather certain sacred objects. These were kept in a bundle or rawhide bag, and hung from a tripod at the back of the lodge, and brought inside at night. Some bundles were hung from lacing pins above the door.

The dreamer was given songs and ceremonies for opening the sacred bundles at set times of the year, always keeping the holy guardian bird or animal in his heart. There were also certain rules for living in the lodge: only family members were allowed to sleep in the Kiowa Hugging Bear Tipi; the fire in the Blackfoot Crow Lodge must never go out; the owner of the Blackfoot Snow Tipi (opposite page) had to purify himself with sweetgrass smoke whenever entering.

Today most of the old dreams are only half remembered, many of the lodge rules nearly forgotten, and too many holy bundles are mere objects of curiosity stacked on dusty museum storage shelves. Most people do not listen to the birds and animals, nor respect the powers of the universe; we are distracted by sports, celebrities, automobiles, and electronic gadgets.

Inside the Blackfoot Snow Lodge
(see also page 42)

Blackfoot Deer Lodge (2000)

This recently painted lodge, above, is most handsome, painted well within the tradition of Blackfoot painted tipis. It has the Bunched Stars and the Seven Persons on the smoke flaps, Morning Star, and dusty stars and hills around the base.

Sadly, the animal drawing of more recent tipis has deteriorated, as this Deer Lodge illustrates when compared with the Antelope Lodge, right. People are no longer dependent on hunting, nor living close to the animals, and the drawings' observation lacks correct body shape, and the spirit, the character of the animals is no longer present.

Blackfoot Antelope Lodge (1900)

Shade
The tipi's cone shape casts only a small shadow for the children to play behind the lodge.

With few trees on the Great Plains, people had to improvise their shade. Umbrellas, decorated with ribbons, feathers, or beadwork, were a popular trade item long before reservation days.

A shade, or wickiup, although probably not often erected during Buffalo Days, is now a structure outside many homes. Four or six forked poles dug into the ground support cross poles upon which pine or leafy branches are laid. The windward side is sometimes closed in with canvas or more branches. The wickiup is the usual summertime place to spend the days, and the coolest place to sleep. It also makes a fine nesting place for the Brewer's Blackbirds.

The Tipi on Hot Days

To let more air into the tipi on hot days, the smoke flaps can be pulled aside, and the poles rested up against the back of the tipi. The cover can be unpegged in parts, rolled, and propped up with forked poles, as shown on the Rainbow Tipi.

When it is too hot to have a fire inside the tipi, cooking is done outside, or else the cover can be simply unpinned and unpegged, and pulled back, as shown with the above Yellow Tipi.

Kiowa Tipis (1870s)
Lone Wolf's Yellow Tipi and Timber Mountain's Rainbow Tipi.

There is a third pole, painted red, propped up against the back of the Rainbow Tipi. Tied to the end was a small rawhide case in which Timber Mountain kept a carved stone buffalo effigy, used in his ceremonies to call the buffalo herds.

Lone Wolf s Yellow Tipi was given to his mother, Necklace, by a visiting party of Arikara who had the tipi cover packed on a dog travois.

Because Lone Wolf had been a leader in the unequal wars against the US military, he was imprisoned in distant Florida for three years. He died the year after he was released.

Parfleches

After the Fall buffalo hunt, great quantities of meat were sliced thinly and hung on racks to dry in the sun, sufficient to last every family through the winter. When dried, the meat was stored in rawhide cases called *parfleches*, which women made and painted in pairs with beautiful geometric designs. When on the move, a pair of parfleches was hung either side of a pack-horse, and in camp they were placed around the edge of the lodge, to keep the tipi lining in place. Parfleches, together with backrests, were the only furniture items that nomadic people carried with them.

Painting a Parfleche

Painting on rawhide was best done when the hide was damp. The lady, in the illustration, has draped an old tipi cover over a tripod of poles for shade to help keep the hide moist. She uses marked sticks to measure and draw straight lines. Her brushes are bones, some porous to paint large areas, others hard and sharp for drawing thin lines.

Later she will cut the hide to the parfleche shape and burn holes so that the case can be tied shut with thongs. Primarily parfleches held dried meat, but also clothes and personal belongings.

Note the small round pebbles tied into the lodge cover. These anchor the peg ties to the canvas and are much stronger than loops sewn to the canvas.

49

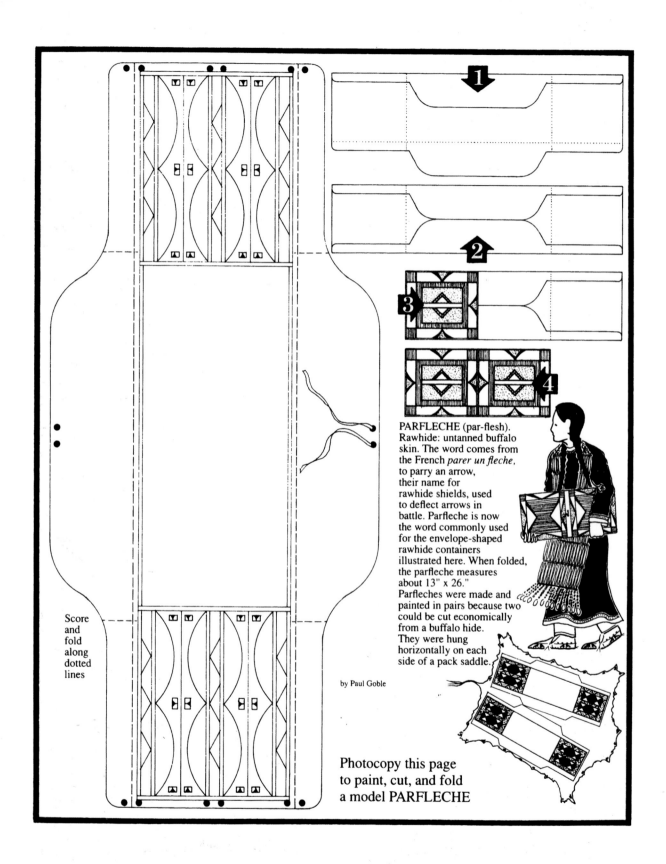

PARFLECHE (par-flesh).
Rawhide: untanned buffalo skin. The word comes from the French *parer un fleche,* to parry an arrow, their name for rawhide shields, used to deflect arrows in battle. Parfleche is now the word commonly used for the envelope-shaped rawhide containers illustrated here. When folded, the parfleche measures about 13" x 26." Parfleches were made and painted in pairs because two could be cut economically from a buffalo hide. They were hung horizontally on each side of a pack saddle.

by Paul Goble

Score and fold along dotted lines

Photocopy this page to paint, cut, and fold a model PARFLECHE

Parfleche Designs

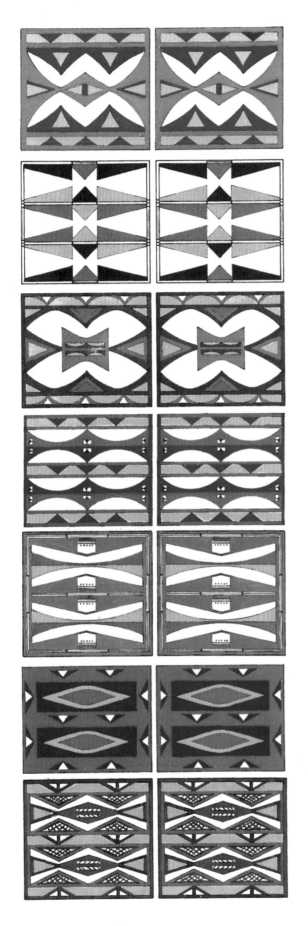

Omaha Tipis

The designs on the opposite page are copied from rough thumbnail sketches made by a missionary to the Omaha people in the early 1870s, by which time the Omaha no longer lived in their former earth lodges or tipis. Even though the sketches were only about the size of these drawings, and drawn from verbal descriptions, we get an idea of the symbols that were important to the Omaha. Traditionally the Omaha had only lived in tipis during the Spring and Fall when they traveled out on the plains in search of the buffalo herds.

As with all painted tipis, each was painted as the result of a dream, and dreamers of the same animal or celestial object formed groups or societies of like-minded people. No person ever thought to paint an object on his tipi which another person had seen in a dream. Here the main elements are bear and buffalo tracks, for those who had dreamed of bears and buffalo, horsetails for horse dreamers, pipes, rainbows, zigzag lightning, the sun, moon, and stars.

An Omaha priest stands by his tipi. He would have helped with the ceremonies and prayers in connection with the twice yearly buffalo hunts, and in planting and harvesting of corn, meat and corn being the staffs of life. Both were spoken of as "Mother," because, like Mother Earth, they provided everything the people needed. This painting was traced from an old (1880s) black-and-white photograph, and so the colors are speculative. Owners of a tipi like this would not have eaten birds, fearing that the relatives of the dead birds would hear about it, and fly down and eat up the crops before they could be harvested.

Gros Ventre Serpent Tipi (1890)

In a dream, Tall Iron Man saw a boy walk out of the water of the Missouri and say to him: "My father invites you to visit him," but Tall Iron Man took no notice of the dream.

He had the same dream the next night, and yet again the night after. "Three is the sacred number," the boy told him. "This is the third time my father asks you to come."

Tall Iron Man got up and followed the boy down to the river. Wading out from the shore into deeper water, the boy stopped and Tall Iron Man saw that they were standing in front of a lodge which had water serpents painted either side of the doorway. Sitting inside at the back was an old man, naked and painted red all over. He gave Tall Iron Man the design of his lodge, together with a pipe which was always to be kept inside the tipi.

When the boy had led Tall Iron Man back home, his family were glad, and told how he had been missing for three days and nights.

Tall Iron Man told this story to an anthropologist, but either fearing ridicule, or not wanting to talk lightly of his dreams, he never told that the dream had been his own.

Zigzag lightning bolts dart from the black storm cloud top of the tipi, the lightning echoed in the jagged edges of the smoke flaps, and the flaps tipped with horse tails, for horses, too, are associated with the thunder and lightning. A fan of eagle tail feathers hangs above each of the monsters' faces, hiding them from casual view. Similar powerful images painted on shields were also sometimes hidden behind bunches of feathers so that the protective power of the images did not evaporate. Here, wind and driving rain reveal the monsters. Each spring the fearful thunder beings wake the monsters from their sleep, to battle and to swell the rivers and flood the land. Each has awesome powers of destruction, yet they also bring water and life to everything.

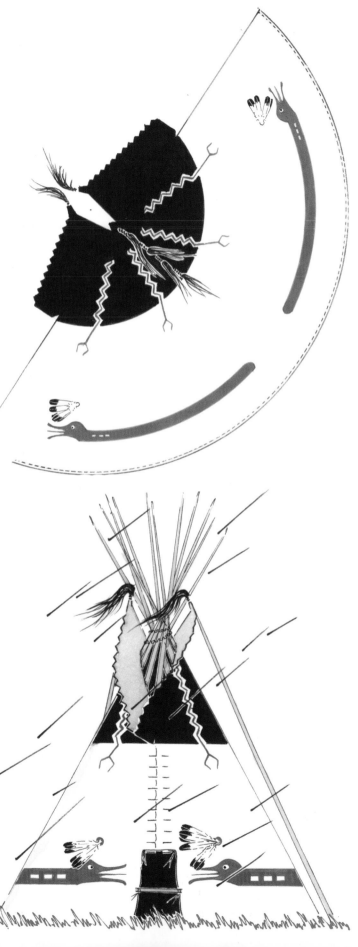

Altars

The altar at the center of the lodge can take many forms. Often it is a small square where the grass has been removed, and the earth finely crumbled and raked smooth. We remember that we and everything come from Mother Earth, and that everything returns to her. This square may be further divided with powdered paint and feathers to mark the Four Winds. This is the center of our home, and our center of the world, and we pray that the Four Winds will be kind to us.

Behind the *owanka wakan*, the sacred place, there may be a forked stick to hang the pipebags, or a rack against which the pipes rest, for it is with the smoke of the sacred pipe that our prayers rise. The alter may simply be a buffalo skull placed on a bed of picked silvery prairie sage, the pipes resting against the skull.

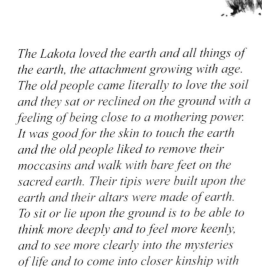

The Lakota loved the earth and all things of the earth, the attachment growing with age. The old people came literally to love the soil and they sat or reclined on the ground with a feeling of being close to a mothering power. It was good for the skin to touch the earth and the old people liked to remove their moccasins and walk with bare feet on the sacred earth. Their tipis were built upon the earth and their altars were made of earth. To sit or lie upon the ground is to be able to think more deeply and to feel more keenly, and to see more clearly into the mysteries of life and to come into closer kinship with other living things.

In talking to children, the old Lakota would place a hand on the ground and explain: "We sit in the lap of our Mother. From her we, and all other living things, come. We shall soon pass, but the place where we now rest will last forever."
Standing Bear, Lakota.

You have noticed that everything an Indian does is in a circle, and that is because the power of the world always works in circles, and everything tries to be round. Everything the power of the world does is done in a circle. The sky is round and so are the stars. The wind, in its greatest power, whirls. Birds make their nests in circles, for theirs is the same religion as ours. The sun comes forth and goes down again in a circle. The moon does the same, and both are round.

Even the seasons form a great circle in their changing and always come back again to where they were. The life of a man is a circle from childhood to childhood and so it is in everything where power moves. Our tipis were round like the nests of birds and these were always set in a circle, the nation's hoop, a nest of many nests where the Great Spirit meant for us to hatch our children.
Black Elk, Lakota.

Lakota Tipis

The tipi, above left, belonged to Nicholas Black Elk. It is copied from 1948 photographs (and differs from the design previously published). When he was nine years old he had a vision in which he was taken up into the sky where the spirits of the world lived in a great tipi. *"I saw the flaming rainbow above the tipi which was built and roofed with cloud and sewed with thongs of lightning."*

To the left of the door Black Elk painted the great black stallion which he also saw: *"He was the chief of all the horses, and when he snorted it was a flash of lightning and his eyes were like the sunset star. He raised his voice and sang. The song he sang was this:*
My horses, prancing they are coming
My horses, prancing they are coming
Prancing, they are coming.
All over the universe they come.
A horse nation, they will dance.
May you behold them.

His voice was not loud, but it went all over the universe and filled it. There was nothing that did not hear, and it was more beautiful than anything can be. It was so beautiful that nothing anywhere could keep from dancing. The virgins danced, and all the circled horses. The leaves on the trees, the grasses on the hills and in the valleys, the waters in the creeks and in the rivers and in the lakes, the four-legged and the two-legged and the wings of the air—all danced together to the music of the stallion's song."

The tipi, above right, is after a painting by the Lakota artist, Andrew Standing Soldier (1930s), and the tipi, below, is from another 1948 photograph.

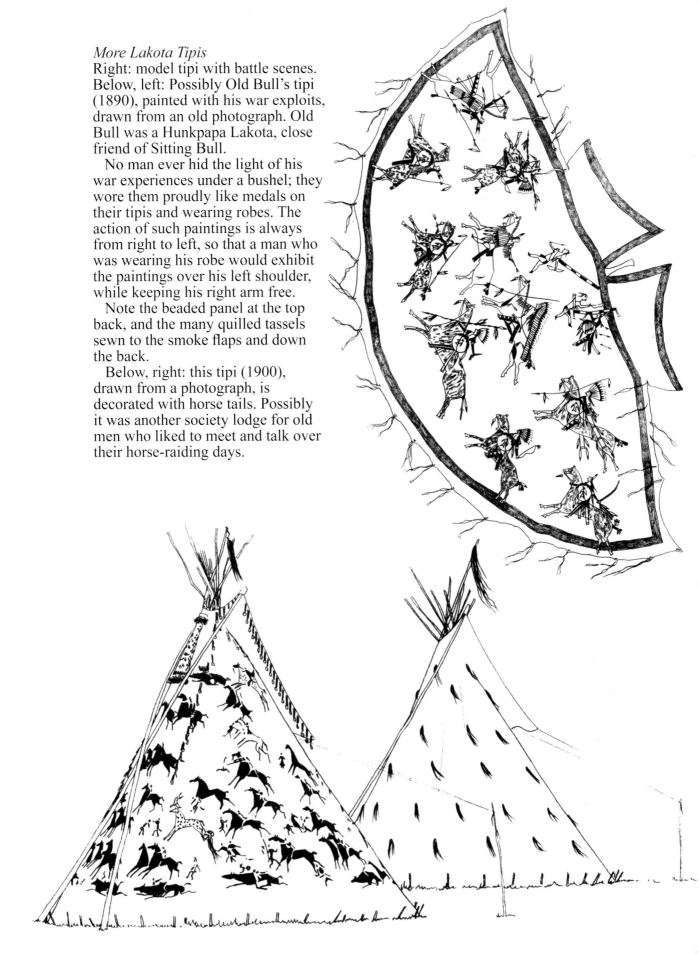

More Lakota Tipis

Right: model tipi with battle scenes.
Below, left: Possibly Old Bull's tipi
(1890), painted with his war exploits,
drawn from an old photograph. Old
Bull was a Hunkpapa Lakota, close
friend of Sitting Bull.

No man ever hid the light of his
war experiences under a bushel; they
wore them proudly like medals on
their tipis and wearing robes. The
action of such paintings is always
from right to left, so that a man who
was wearing his robe would exhibit
the paintings over his left shoulder,
while keeping his right arm free.

Note the beaded panel at the top
back, and the many quilled tassels
sewn to the smoke flaps and down
the back.

Below, right: this tipi (1900),
drawn from a photograph, is
decorated with horse tails. Possibly
it was another society lodge for old
men who liked to meet and talk over
their horse-raiding days.

Miniconjou Lakota Tipi Circle

White Bull pictured the ceremonial tipi circle of his Miniconjou people. He was 81 years old when he wrote:

"A long time ago there were many chiefs in the Miniconjou sub-band, but only a few are left. There were many good men among them, friend. They dried a lot of meat and hung it up. This was buffalo meat."

White Bull drew the meat hanging to dry on racks between the tipis. His lodge was the all red one:

"White Bull's tipi, he is chief."

In this copy of his drawing, we can see more Lakota tipi designs.

White Bull's Tipi

White Bull drew the tipi which he and his wife made when they were young. He added these nostalgic words:

"This is a picture of the buffalo-hide tipi in which I lived. I was living in it the summer they were fighting with the Crow Indians across a body of water (1875). The poles you see we cut at White Mountain. I was with my wife cutting these tipi poles. The buffalo I shot and three women tanned them. They were good seamstresses, my friend. For a good tipi of this sort twenty-two poles were required, friend. I was twenty-five years old at the time. I had a fine lodge and seventeen horses of my own. It was good, my friend. Chief White Bull."

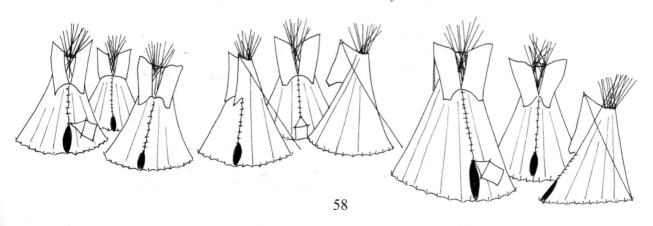

58

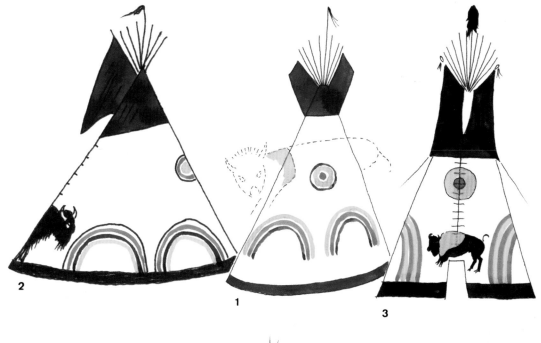

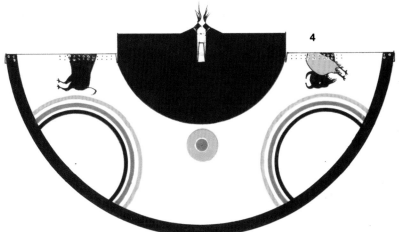

Chief Red Cloud's Tipi

Red Cloud's tipi is one of only a few Lakota tipi designs that has come down to us from Buffalo Days. He was the great Lakota leader who defeated the US soldiers at the Fetterman Fight, and drove the military out of his Powder River country in present-day Wyoming.

Above are copies of three renderings of the chief's painted tipi: #1 and #2 were painted on leather, now indistinct with age, probably by the chiefs son, Jack Red Cloud, in the early 1900s. #3 was painted by Amos Bad Heart Bull, Lakota historian, in his ledger book at about the same time.

#4 is how the tipi might have looked, incorporating the powerful symbols for a great man: red sun with yellow halo, blue or black night sky top and bottom border, rainbows either side, and over the doorway the figure of a buffalo with a yellow hump, indicating winter hair not yet shed. All three renderings indicate a horse tail or scalp attached to the tip of the lifting pole.

Flag of the Oglala Lakota Nation

59

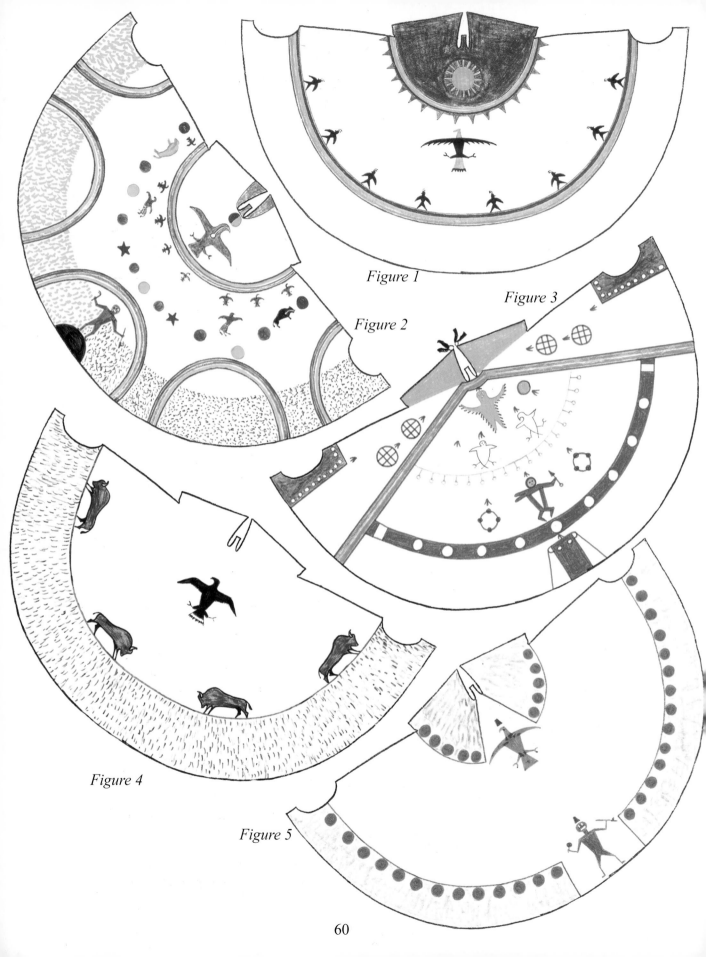

Figure 1

Figure 2

Figure 3

Figure 4

Figure 5

60

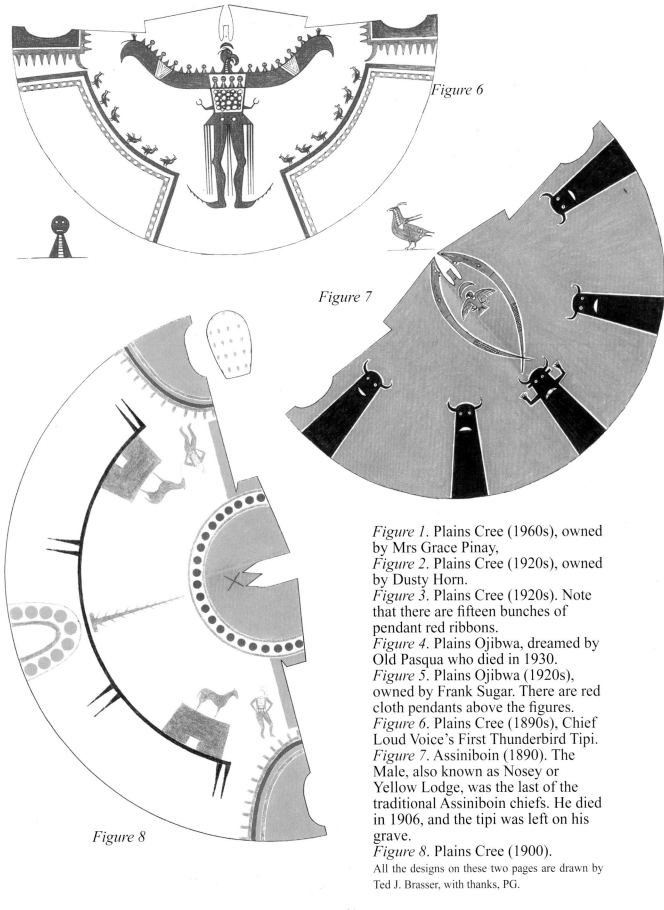

Figure 6

Figure 7

Figure 8

Figure 1. Plains Cree (1960s), owned by Mrs Grace Pinay,
Figure 2. Plains Cree (1920s), owned by Dusty Horn.
Figure 3. Plains Cree (1920s). Note that there are fifteen bunches of pendant red ribbons.
Figure 4. Plains Ojibwa, dreamed by Old Pasqua who died in 1930.
Figure 5. Plains Ojibwa (1920s), owned by Frank Sugar. There are red cloth pendants above the figures.
Figure 6. Plains Cree (1890s), Chief Loud Voice's First Thunderbird Tipi.
Figure 7. Assiniboin (1890). The Male, also known as Nosey or Yellow Lodge, was the last of the traditional Assiniboin chiefs. He died in 1906, and the tipi was left on his grave.
Figure 8. Plains Cree (1900).

All the designs on these two pages are drawn by Ted J. Brasser, with thanks, PG.

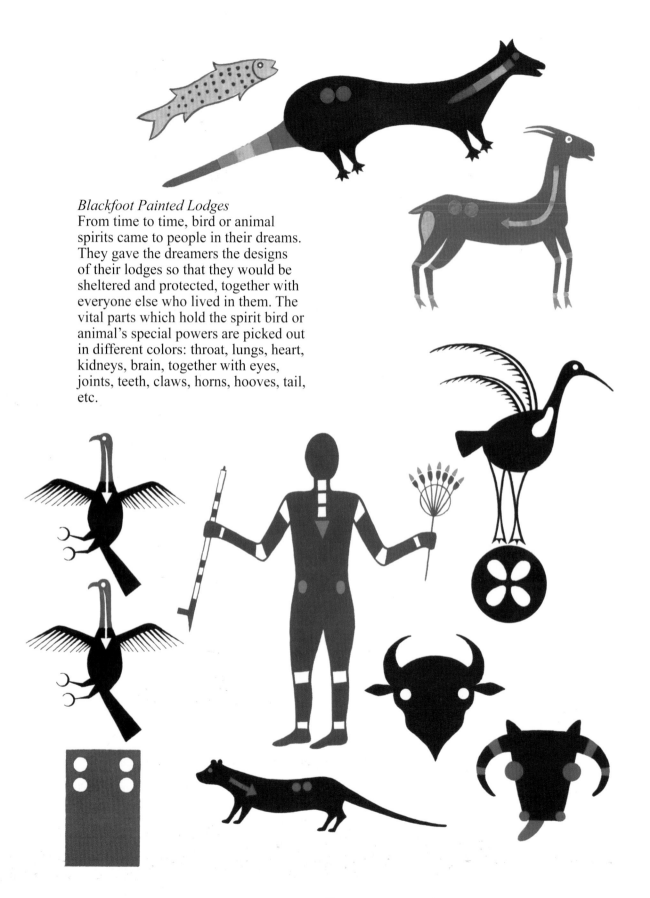

Blackfoot Painted Lodges
From time to time, bird or animal
spirits came to people in their dreams.
They gave the dreamers the designs
of their lodges so that they would be
sheltered and protected, together with
everyone else who lived in them. The
vital parts which hold the spirit bird or
animal's special powers are picked out
in different colors: throat, lungs, heart,
kidneys, brain, together with eyes,
joints, teeth, claws, horns, hooves, tail,
etc.

Some Meanings of Blackfoot Lodge Designs

The poles stretching above the tipi are the pathways along which our hopes and prayers pass up to the Above World. Sky and earth meet where the poles join.

The top of the lodge is the sky, our Father, who with the sun, lightning, and rain brings life to the earth. The painted top is the day or night sky, with discs for the Seven Stars (Dipper), usually on the north smoke flap, the Bunched Stars, Lost Children (Pleiades), on the south.

This Otter Lodge has four single stars marking the Four Winds.

The cross at the back, near the top, can either be the moth who brings good dreams, or Morning Star (Venus) who brings wisdom.

Bands below the top may be clouds, rainbows, spirit trails, or in the case of this lodge, ripples upon the water where the otters live.

The bottom border is the earth, our Mother, with level plains, projecting rounded hills, as in this lodge, or pointed mountains. Within the border are "dusty" or "fallen" stars; these are puff-balls that appear so mysteriously in the grass overnight. Depending on the lodge design, discs can also be hailstones, rocks, or ponds.

The large projections above the bottom border at the back and front of this Otter Lodge, are doorways: the front projection is the doorway where we enter the otters' lodge; the one at the back is the doorway where the spirit otters enter the lodge to protect us.

The main area of the lodge, between the sky and the earth border, is the world of the spirit birds and animals who gave the lodge designs to the dreamer.

Front View

Back View

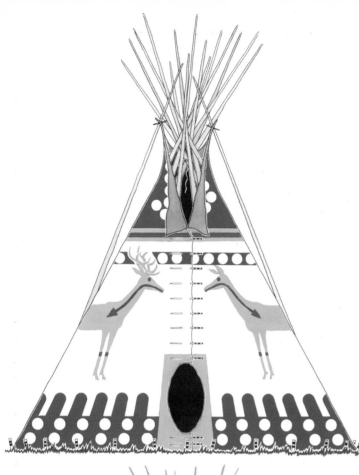

Two Blackfoot Elk Lodges
Top: a 1940s lodge.
Bottom: copied from an old (1900s) photograph. Color not known.

The Blackfoot prefer to use the word "lodge" because "tipi" is a Lakota word. "Blackfoot" is here used to include the three peoples, Piegan, Blood, and Blackfoot.

In both designs it can be seen that the bull elk is painted on the south side, the cow elk on the north. The tradition for painting male animals on the south sides of tipis and females on the north seems to have been universal, but the reason is not understood. Men sit on the north sides of lodges, close to the female animals; women sit and cook on the south side, close to the male animals.

There were several Elk Lodges in the Blackfoot villages, each with a different story of its gift.

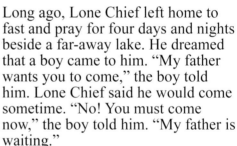

Long ago, Lone Chief left home to fast and pray for four days and nights beside a far-away lake. He dreamed that a boy came to him. "My father wants you to come," the boy told him. Lone Chief said he would come sometime. "No! You must come now," the boy told him. "My father is waiting."

The boy led Lone Chief down to the shore of the lake. "Close your eyes!" he told Lone Chief, and when he told him to open his eyes again, he was standing inside an elk painted lodge. The owner invited him to sit beside him. "I have heard you praying, Lone Chief," the man said, "and I feel sorry for your suffering. I give you my lodge. If you look after it, and faithfully carry out the ceremonies, which I will teach you, and never kill my elk children, then your prayers will be answered."

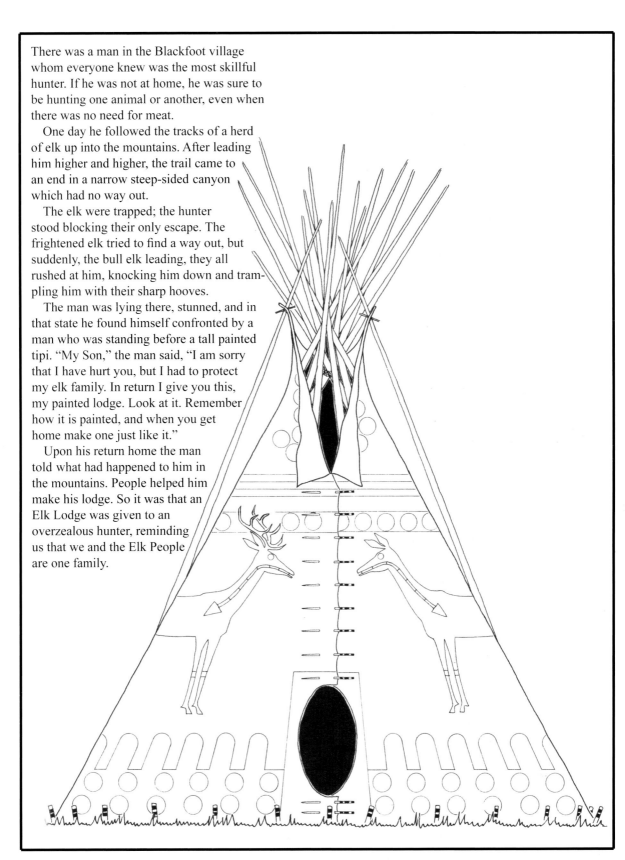

There was a man in the Blackfoot village whom everyone knew was the most skillful hunter. If he was not at home, he was sure to be hunting one animal or another, even when there was no need for meat.

One day he followed the tracks of a herd of elk up into the mountains. After leading him higher and higher, the trail came to an end in a narrow steep-sided canyon which had no way out.

The elk were trapped; the hunter stood blocking their only escape. The frightened elk tried to find a way out, but suddenly, the bull elk leading, they all rushed at him, knocking him down and trampling him with their sharp hooves.

The man was lying there, stunned, and in that state he found himself confronted by a man who was standing before a tall painted tipi. "My Son," the man said, "I am sorry that I have hurt you, but I had to protect my elk family. In return I give you this, my painted lodge. Look at it. Remember how it is painted, and when you get home make one just like it."

Upon his return home the man told what had happened to him in the mountains. People helped him make his lodge. So it was that an Elk Lodge was given to an overzealous hunter, reminding us that we and the Elk People are one family.

BLACKFOOT ELK LODGE
—Photocopy this page to color—

How the *Snake Lodge* was received is told in the ancient adventures of Blood Clot Boy. He is the handsome young man who never grows old, and who for all time travels the world seeking to help people in need.

One time he found an old man and woman who were starving because giant snakes, living in a nearby lake, stole all their meat. Blood Clot Boy fought and killed the snakes with his white stone knife. In the battle, all the water splashed out of the lake, and today the lake bed is dry, and the rocks the color of blood. Similarly the lodge is the color of blood.

Note that the male snake has a single horn on his head. The circles, front and back of the lodge, are the snakes' dens. Because Blood Clot Boy had found the snakes in possession of so much meat, those who live in the lodge always have plenty of meat.

The *Striped Lodge* was given to a man called Blackfoot Child. The people were camped near the Sweet Grass Hills in Alberta searching for the buffalo herds. Blackfoot Child had a dream that he entered a tipi with stripes painted around it. The owner asked him, "Blackfoot Child, do you know where you are?" He replied that he did not. "You are right among the buffalo herds," the lodge owner told him. "The stripes around my lodge are the many paths which the buffaloes make walking to and fro, here and there. In return for visiting me I give you my lodge. Paint yours like mine, and you will always know you are among the buffalo herds."

There are several striped lodges in the Blackfoot camps.

Calf Robe's Lodge
It is a surprise to see in an Alberta tipi circle a flag pole erected in front of a tipi. Queen Victoria presented a flag to forebears of the Calf Robe family and it is still flown today.

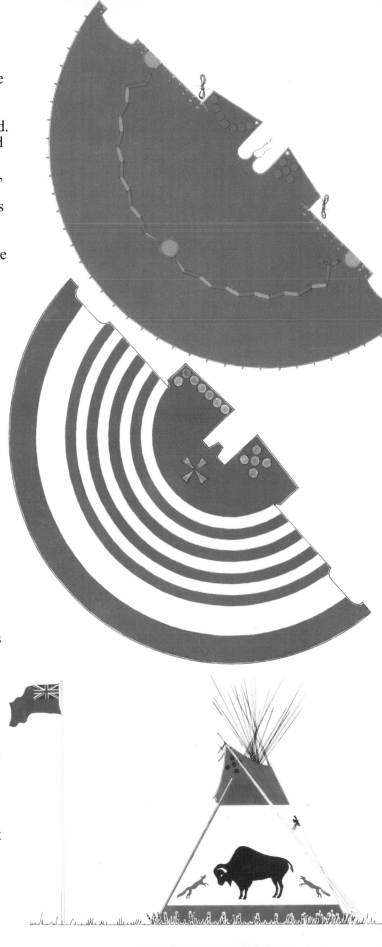

Blackfoot Striped Lodge (1970s), Otter Lodge (1950s), Snake Lodge (1940s), Eagle Lodge (1940s).

Blackfoot Eagle Lodge

A young man named Bad Roads went into the mountains to fast and pray. He dreamed that a man came and took him to his tipi. The man told him, "I am the leader of the Eagles. I have brought you to my lodge so you can see the drawings on it. Look carefully and make one just like it." The Eagle man also taught Bad Roads the right way to catch eagles for their sacred feathers.

The meaning of the striking wavy lines has been forgotten; they may represent the mountains where the eagles live, or possibly their undulating flights. Below these are the level plains with dusty stars.

The *Otter Lodge*, above, has an otter skin "flag" hanging atop the lifting pole. The bottom border of the lodge has rounded hills, and at the top a starry sky with Morning Star at the back.

67

Blackfoot Big Rock Lodge (1900)
There are colossal glacial boulders at the base of the northern Rocky Mountains in Blackfoot Country. Buffalo, and surely mammoths before them, would gather round the boulders for shade or protection from the wind, and to scratch their sides.

Note the buffalo wool on the smoke flaps, associating the idea of the shed buffalo hair found around those boulders. This lodge, like some of the oldest designs, has no Morning Star, or constellations on the smoke flaps.

In winter camps, logs or rocks were used to weigh down the cover to keep out drafts, as shown here, while leaving enough air to enter under the cover to draw the smoke from the lodge. Logs would rot the cover, making it necessary to either renew the cover, or to trim the bottom, which left a smaller lodge.

The Distant Blackfoot Lodges
Some of the lodges, above left, can
be identified: Horse Lodge, (note the
horse tail hanging from the center
of the Morning Star), Buffalo Head
Lodge, Snow Lodge, Crow Lodge
and a Striped Lodge, all from the
1900s.

Above right: three Otter Lodges
(1990s), and the Black Buffalo
Lodge, (1960s, see page 71).

Blackfoot Buffalo Head Lodge
(1940s)
In summer camps, leafy branches
were sometimes placed round the
bottom of the lodge, as painted
here, helping to keep out dust, and
preventing uninvited dogs pushing
under the cover. On very hot days
large leafy branches might be cut
and leaned against the cover for
shade.

69

Painting the Yellow Buffalo Lodge
In this modern scene, with proper ceremonial observed for painting a new tipi, the cover is staked to the ground to prevent the canvas shrinking when water and commercial paints are applied. Coffee cans or aluminum pie pans are convenient templates for the stars.

Black Buffalo Lodge (1960s) and the Yellow Buffalo Lodge (1900s)
Note that the figure on the Yellow Buffalo Lodge has two eyes on one side of its head. This is the old painting convention, to show what is known as well as what is seen.

These two tipis are also known as the Yellow-Painted and the Black-Painted Buffalo-Stone Lodges. Buffalo stones, *iniskims*, were kept in these tipis, and used by holy men in the ceremonies to call the buffaloes when the people needed meat. Both of the lodges, and the *iniskims* were gifts from the underwater spirits:

Long ago, two young men, Weasel Heart and Fisher, also known as Most Sacred Man, were brother friends, sworn to defend each other and their families. One day they were sitting on a high bank overlooking Bow River, making arrows from chokecherry shoots.

Weasel Heart, looking down into the river which was in spate, could hardly believe what he saw. He said to his friend, "Do you see the top of that lodge and its poles sticking out of the water down there?" Fisher saw the lodge. "Yes, I see it," he replied, "and I see another lodge close to it." Weasel Heart saw that one too.

Each waited on the bank while the other dived down to receive the lodge from the underwater spirits. These were the Yellow and Black Buffalo Lodges.

Some years later, when the river was again in spate, the people wanted to cross, but it was too dangerous. Even so Weasel Heart swam across. Then he and Fisher walked into the river from opposite sides, and as they approached each other in the middle, the water went down. The people all crossed safely. It has been a shallow crossing place ever since, known as Blackfoot Crossing on Bow River in southern Alberta.

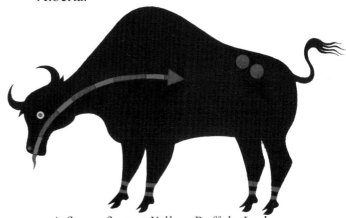

A figure from a *Yellow Buffalo Lodge* Lodge of the 1940s

71

Blackfoot Lodges

Left to right:
Buffalo Hoof Lodge (1940s). *Snake Lodge* (1970s; See page 66). Another *Buffalo Hoof Lodge* (1970s; see also cover at left). *Curlew Lodge* (1940s). Another *Snake Lodge* (1970s), opposite page.

Big Rock Lodge (1970s). The rocks painted on the back and front of the lodge look more like huge red suns. (See also opposite page.) This design has not changed from photographs taken in the early 1900s, and no doubt the design existed back in Buffalo Days. (See another Big Rock Lodge, page 68.)

Bear Lodge (1970s). This is another lodge with an ancient pedigree. The red circles represent the bears' den in which a young man had entered to fast and pray for four days and nights, seeking spiritual guidance and protection in battle.

While sleeping, the bears came to him and promised that they would always protect him. In battle, they told him, he should charge the enemy, just like they charged their enemies.

The mother bear gave him a knife, throwing it at him, which he caught. She also gave him a song to sing in battle: *A knife is just like dirt thrown at me*, meaning that he need have no more fear of weapons than of dirt.

They showed him how he should cover his face with paint before going into battle, and then with his fingers to scratch off some of the paint in vertical lines down his face like bear claw marks.

Otter Lodge (1970s).
Antelope Lodge (1970s).
Hugging Lodge (see page 80).
Striped Lodge (see page 66).

Council Tipi
If a tipi was not large enough for everyone to take part in an important discussion, the cover was unpegged, rolled and propped up with forked sticks. This is the Big Rock Lodge.

Sarsi Peace Pipe Lodge of Big Belly
This lodge has the same general design concept as the Skunk Lodge which is illustrated on page 1. About 1870, both designs were given by a snake in a dream to Big Belly, an important medicine man.

Although the Sarsi are closely associated with the Blackfeet, they kept their identity, and their lodges did not fit within the Blackfoot tradition of painted tipis, as these two designs illustrate.

In addition to the skunks coming down the front of the lodge (page 1) there was a skunk standing atop the spirit door at the back of the lodge.

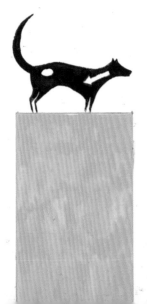

At one time the Blackfoot, too, had a Skunk Lodge, although no visual record of it remains. About 1850 a party of Blood Indians were ambushed and the only survivor was Scalp Robe who escaped by hiding under a rock. He remained there for a long time in fear of his life, when he fell asleep. He dreamed that he approached a tipi and that someone inside invited him to enter. It was a Skunk Person who told him that he need not be afraid because he would protect him so that he would return home safely. The Skunk Person gave him the design of his tipi, which had skunks painted on both sides, and down the back, and there were seven crows below the painted top.

When Scalp Robe had made the lodge as he had seen it in his dream, he invited everyone to a feast. Scalp Robe was wearing a skunk skin cap, and people began to whisper that the cap seemed to be alive. Scalp Robe suddenly threw the cap on the ground, they say, and it became a live skunk running around among the guests and spraying them with its terrible smell. End of feast, but ever after that everyone knew that Scalp Robe had received powerful help indeed from the skunk.

Dipper and Pleiades Constellations
In the tradition of Blackfoot painted tipis, the Big Dipper and Pleiades are usually painted on the smoke flaps: the Dipper on the north smoke flap (below right), because that is the direction in which we see those stars, the Pleiades on the south (below left), although this order is often reversed. Below are some of the many forms in which these constellations are painted, and ways to show the flag.

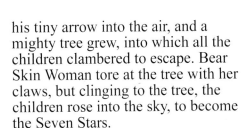

In the sacred stories of the Blackfoot, the Pleiades are called the Lost Children or the Bunched Stars. The story tells that at one time the poor and orphaned children were so neglected, going about in ragged clothes and hungry, that they they did not want to be children any longer. The dogs were their only friends. They decided they wanted to be stars because stars are always beautiful.

One of the children who had power blew a feather into the air and, together with the dogs, they rose into the sky to become the stars of the Lost Children. Painted on nearly every tipi is this reminder to look after all the little children.

The Seven Stars, the Big Dipper, were also children at one time: six brothers, together with their sister, *Sinopa*, who carried her baby brother, *Okinai*, on her back, were playing one day. They were joined by their oldest sister, Bear Skin Woman. Suddenly she changed into a bear and chased them. Little *Okinai* shot his tiny arrow into the air, and a mighty tree grew, into which all the children clambered to escape. Bear Skin Woman tore at the tree with her claws, but clinging to the tree, the children rose into the sky, to become the Seven Stars.

Sinopa still carries little *Okinai* on her back. Look carefully and you will see there are really eight stars. White people know her as *Mizar*, and her baby brother, *Alcor*. The stump of that great tree, with its bear claw slashes from top to bottom, can be seen in northwest Wyoming. White people call it Devil's Tower, but for Indian peoples there is no Devil; they call it Bear Lodge Butte.

Blackfoot Fish Lodge (1940)
There was a boy in the village called One Spot who liked to spend his days at the river catching fish. Day after day it was the same, and at evening he would bring home his catch and give it to his parents or grandparents, uncles and aunts, and they were all proud of him.

One night as One Spot slept, a man came to him. "Get up, my Son, and follow after me," the man told him. He led One Spot down to the river where there was a beautiful painted tipi that One Spot had never seen before, with spotted fishes at the doorway. The top was colored the red sky of dawn, and below it, ripples and green water weed.

"My Son," the man said, "I have brought you here to tell you that I am sad because you have been killing all my fish children. I will give you my tipi, but in return I ask you to promise never to kill any more of my children."

One Spot promised, and those who live in the Fish Lodge do not kill or eat fish.

76

Blackfoot Beaver Lodge (1950s)
The large red door surround represents the beavers' lodge, and the doorway through which people enter the beavers' own lodge. There is an identical painted lodge at the back of the tipi which is the doorway for the spirit beavers.

Seven Stars are on the north smoke flap; the black line below the red top, a ripple on the beavers' pond.

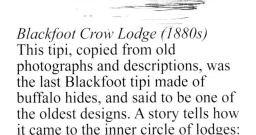

Blackfoot Crow Lodge (1880s)
This tipi, copied from old photographs and descriptions, was the last Blackfoot tipi made of buffalo hides, and said to be one of the oldest designs. A story tells how it came to the inner circle of lodges:

A man was so admired because of his success in capturing horses from the enemy, that the leader of the village felt his position was threatened. By casting a spell, he brought bad luck on the man, who after that always returned home unsuccessful.

Walking home a fourth time, tired out, he killed a buffalo. When he had made an offering of meat, he sat down by his fire to eat and rest.

While sleeping a man came to him and said: "Again I see you walking home, my Son. I, too, travel great distances searching for food, but you have just given meat to me and my crow children. After this you will know that I shall always be close to you for I will help you to become the leader of your people. I give you my lodge; never let the fire go out, and burn sweet grass in its coals morning and evening and purify yourself in its smoke. Now, go back and you will find horses, and from today you need never walk again."

The man foretold truly for he became the leader of his village.

Each of the 14 crows on the tipi cover has a piece of red cloth in its beak, representing buffalo meat.

Blackfoot Lodges

Some Blackfoot painted tipis are without figures. The cover, right, has an ancient lineage, and is known as a Buffalo Trails Lodge.

At one time a man went to fast and pray in the Sweetgrass Hills. He had a dream in which an old man and woman, who were the leaders of the buffalo people, gave him their tipi. The four bands around the top of their lodge, they told the dreamer, were the trails of the male and female buffalo.

The man later received a stone which helped him to find the buffalo herds when people needed meat. This stone, it is said, gave birth to other stones, and these he gave away, which is why there are other Buffalo Trails Lodges in the Blackfoot villages. The large painted projection at the back of the lodge, either represents the buffalo stone, or the spirit door for the leader of the buffalo and his wife to enter the lodge.

Very occasionally, walking on the prairie, a person may hear a sweet bird-like sound. At that place, it is said, if a person looks carefully, may be found a lucky buffalo stone, an *iniskim*. (These appear to be smooth fossil bones, about two inches long, somewhat in the shape of a buffalo.)

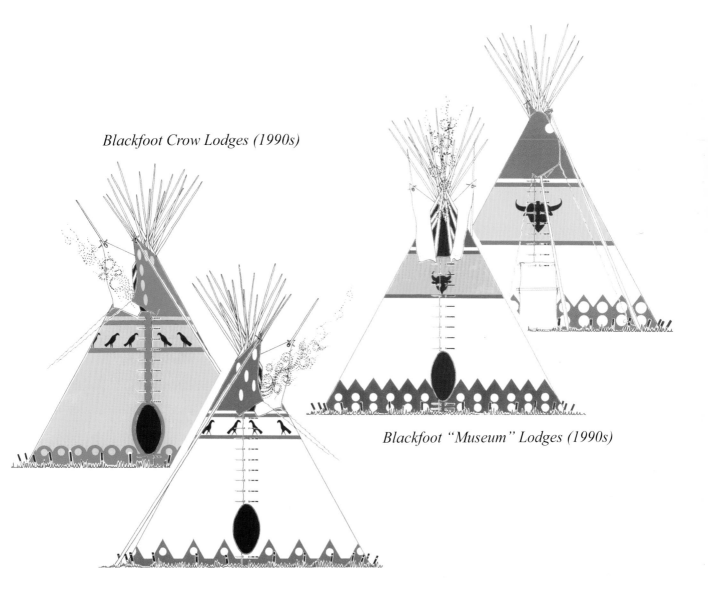

Blackfoot Crow Lodges (1990s)

Blackfoot "Museum" Lodges (1990s)

Crow and Buffalo Head Lodges
The lodges on these two pages are beautiful and yet they are examples of how the tradition is breaking down, painted in duplicates and for exhibitions.

The two Crow Lodges were painted by the same person in the early 1990s. They seem to be painted more as "art," experimenting with shapes and colors: rounded hills on one, pointed mountains on the other; red and white for one, the other yellow and blue; six stars on the north smoke flap, where there is usually the Seven Stars, the Big Dipper.

(Note that this detail so worried the illustrator of these pages, that in the distant Crow Lodge, on the opposite page, he added a star to make seven!)

The Buffalo Head Lodges are today's typical museum Blackfoot tipi exhibit, evidently all painted by the same person.

Note that the Crow Lodge smoke flaps are set for a north wind on one, south wind on the other. One of the Buffalo Head Lodges, above, has the smoke flaps tightly closed against a hard rain. Obviously there can be no fire inside!

79

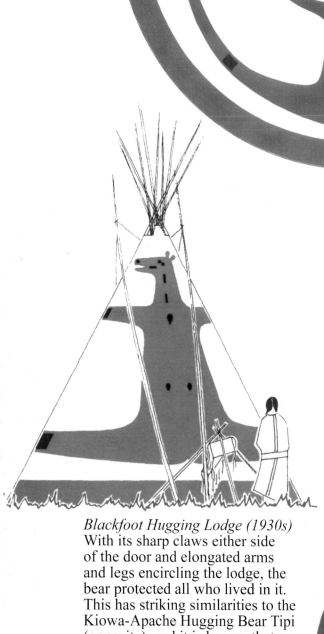

Blackfoot Hugging Lodge (1930s)
With its sharp claws either side of the door and elongated arms and legs encircling the lodge, the bear protected all who lived in it. This has striking similarities to the Kiowa-Apache Hugging Bear Tipi (opposite), and it is known that a Cheyenne named Whirlwind had a similar lodge. Unlike the Kiowa-Apache, the Blackfoot never refer to the lodge as the Hugging Bear Lodge, but call it the Hugging Lodge, or just Hugging. Bears are held in too much awe to mention them by name. Note that as in the old style of painting, both eyes are painted on one side of the head.

One day when the people were moving from place to place looking for the buffalo herds, a little boy wandered off when his mother was busy and was lost. A bear found him, and took him to his den for his wife and children to look after, like one of the family. Several years later when his people came again to the same place, the boy returned home bearing gifts from his bear family, one of which was the design of the Hugging Lodge.

Note the tripod at the back of the lodge: hanging from it are rawhide bags containing sacred objects belonging to the tipi, some of them gifts from the bears, long ago.

Bears From Other Blackfoot Lodges

Hugging Bear Tipi, Kiowa-Apache (1860s)

In a dream Lone Chief saw a great bear hugging a tipi. "Make this tipi," the bear told him, "and I shall always hold you up."

A person could not have any greater protection than that of the awesome bear. Bears also give medicines because they know about roots, plants, and berries, and those who lived in the tipi were given that knowledge. One of the rules of the lodge was that if any family member was sick, he or she would recover if another family member promised to replace the cover when it was worn out. The old cover was abandoned in a remote place, staked to the ground with the bear's head facing the rising sun.

The vertical lines on the red background are the claw markings bears leave on trees to mark their territory. Strips of red tradecloth are sewn to the smoke flap pockets. The door is a bear skin with the hair removed, but left around the edges.

The night had been hot; the girls had taken their blankets outside to sleep. Now the sun is rising, and the badger and jack rabbit will find somewhere to sleep.

81

Kiowa and Kiowa-Apache Tipis

Around 1895, James Mooney, an ethnologist at the Smithsonian Institution in Washington, DC, wished to recreate for an exhibit the Kiowa and Kiowa-Apache Sun Dance tipi circle of 238 tipis, of which about fifty, one in five, would have been painted. These were to be exact models, each a little over two feet high. Although the project was never completed, the more than thirty tipi designs which were made, constitute the most complete record of painted tipis of any group of Indian peoples.

At the time these models were made, the Kiowa and Kiowa-Apache were no longer living in tipis, and only one painted tipi existed. The original tipis for these models had not been seen for thirty years and more. Each of the designs on the pages which follow (and the Cheyenne tipis which follow after these, because Mooney had the same idea for the Cheyenne) was proudly remembered by family descendants of the original owners, and painted by young Kiowa men. The Kiowa and Kiowa-Apache peoples numbered only around 1250, and being closely knit, everyone knowing everyone else, and under Mooney's encouragement, the designs were clearly remembered and saved from falling into oblivion.

Kiowa-Apache Tipi of Standing Among Men

Here are two large rainbows against a yellow background, and a fringed sun at the back. Sadly, nothing is known about the man and the boy, possibly father and son, who are offering a sacred pipe in prayer.

No information can be found about the handsome Kiowa-Apache tipis on the opposite page. It is interesting that seven of the eight favor following the bold geometry of the tipi poles, and that only three of the eight have door cutouts. Unlike the Blackfoot and Cheyenne, the Kiowa and Kiowa-Apache include the door as part of the tipi's design, giving it a matching or contrasting color.

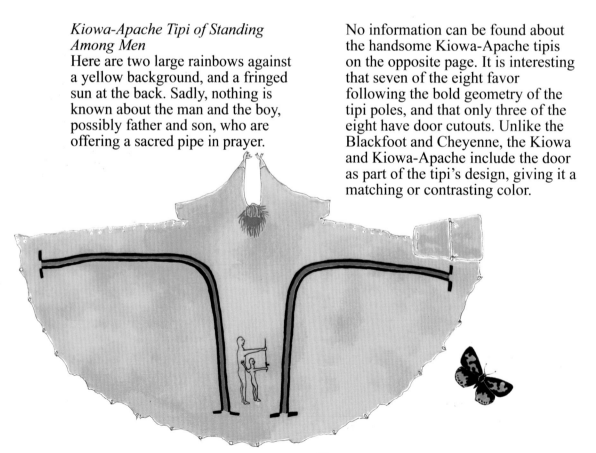

Kiowa-Apache Tipis

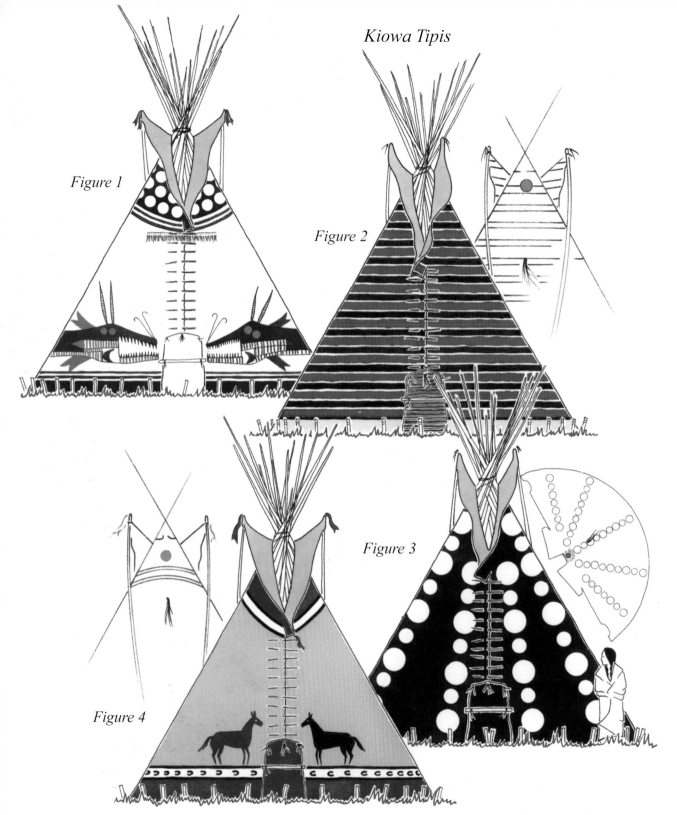

Figure 1

Figure 2

Figure 3

Figure 4

Figure 1. Horned Fish Tipi
The fearsome Horned Fish, above and opposite, is the same as the Under-Water Monster. Although rarely seen, they drowned weak swimmers and hung their scalps on their horns as trophies! Note the rainbow borders, the thundercloud top filled with hailstones, and fringes for rain, because the thunderbirds battle eternally with the under-water monsters.

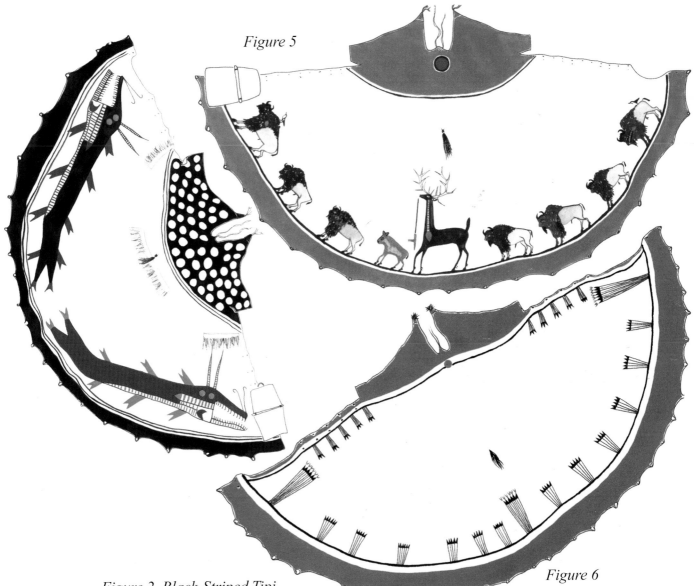

Figure 5

Figure 6

Figure 2. Black-Striped Tipi
This has fifteen red and sixteen black stripes, and a striped door. Stripes often meant successful paths against the enemy. It was quite common that people came to be known by the name of their tipi, and two generations who owned this lodge were each known as Black-Striped Tipi Man.

Figure 3. Howling Elk's Black Tipi
Here there are stars against a black sky, and a green fringed leather sun at the top back.

Figure 4. Crazy Bear's Horse Tipi
Crazy Bear received this lodge as a gift from an Arapaho man in the early 1800s. Note the horse tracks entering the tipi. The buffalo tail at the back is a feature of almost every

Kiowa and Kiowa-Apache tipi, and was surely an affirmation that people and buffalo were closely related.

Figure 5. Buffalo Tipi of Never Got Shot
Six buffalo bulls, a cow, calf, and an elk, but no story of this lodge is known. The birds perched on the backs of the bulls either side of the door are probably yellow-headed blackbirds.

Figure 6. Big Bow's Tail Tipi
Big Bow, wise man and war leader, inherited this lodge. Here are many eagle tail feather fans, the smallest bright blue sun, and buffalo wool on the tips of the smoke flaps.

85

Figure 1

Figure 2

Figure 3

Figure 4

Figure 5

Figure 6

Figure 7

Figure 8

Kiowa Tipis

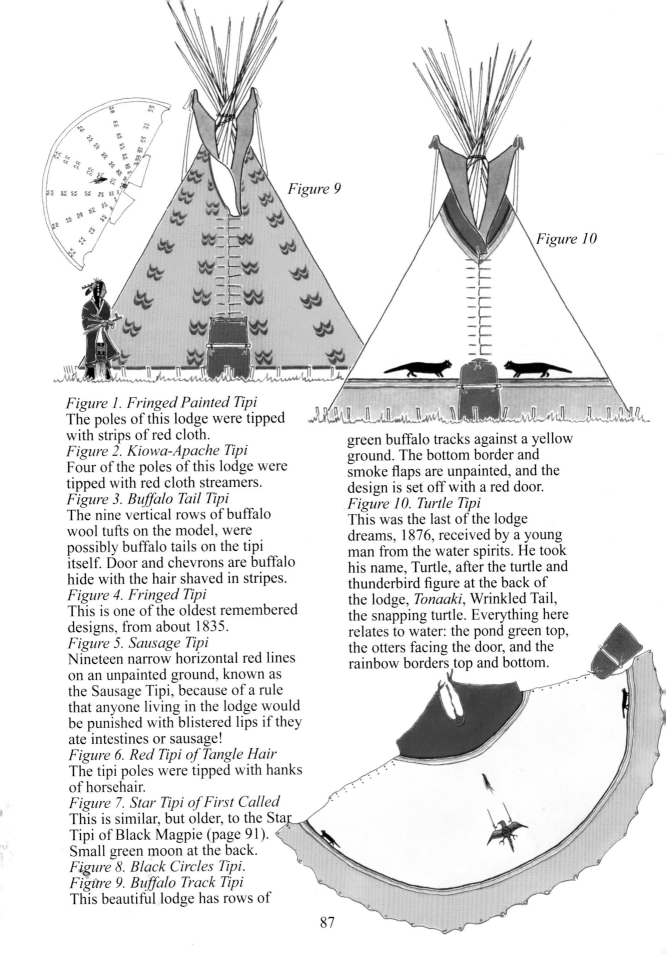

Figure 9

Figure 10

Figure 1. Fringed Painted Tipi
The poles of this lodge were tipped with strips of red cloth.
Figure 2. Kiowa-Apache Tipi
Four of the poles of this lodge were tipped with red cloth streamers.
Figure 3. Buffalo Tail Tipi
The nine vertical rows of buffalo wool tufts on the model, were possibly buffalo tails on the tipi itself. Door and chevrons are buffalo hide with the hair shaved in stripes.
Figure 4. Fringed Tipi
This is one of the oldest remembered designs, from about 1835.
Figure 5. Sausage Tipi
Nineteen narrow horizontal red lines on an unpainted ground, known as the Sausage Tipi, because of a rule that anyone living in the lodge would be punished with blistered lips if they ate intestines or sausage!
Figure 6. Red Tipi of Tangle Hair
The tipi poles were tipped with hanks of horsehair.
Figure 7. Star Tipi of First Called
This is similar, but older, to the Star Tipi of Black Magpie (page 91). Small green moon at the back.
Figure 8. Black Circles Tipi.
Figure 9. Buffalo Track Tipi
This beautiful lodge has rows of

green buffalo tracks against a yellow ground. The bottom border and smoke flaps are unpainted, and the design is set off with a red door.
Figure 10. Turtle Tipi
This was the last of the lodge dreams, 1876, received by a young man from the water spirits. He took his name, Turtle, after the turtle and thunderbird figure at the back of the lodge, *Tonaaki*, Wrinkled Tail, the snapping turtle. Everything here relates to water: the pond green top, the otters facing the door, and the rainbow borders top and bottom.

Daveko's Moon Tipi, Kiowa-Apache (1850s)

Daveko's Moon Tipi, Kiowa-Apache (1850s)

Daveko had been invited to be a member of a society of the very bravest men among his people, and on an occasion when the members had met and danced for four days and nights, Daveko collapsed with exhaustion on his way home. He dreamed that he saw this tipi, and a voice told him that it would never blow down, not even in the fiercest of winds. Furthermore, the voice told him, he had nothing to fear, for he would only die when he was very old.

In this painting, the smoke flaps have been crossed and closed tight against the approaching storm. The design, seen here from the back, repeats on the front of the lodge. Bunches of sacred sweet grass are tied to the points of the crescent moons.

That wind! That wind!
Shakes my tipi!
Shakes my tipi!
And sings a song for me.
Kiowa.

A Kiowa named Fair-Haired Old Man received this *Eagle Tipi* design in a vision about 1830. He gave the design to his friend, Sheathed Lance, in 1851, and in 1900 this model was made for the Smithsonian Institution by Sheathed Lance's daughter who remembered the design.

There are fifteen eagles on the north side, and forty-six stars on the south, with rainbow lines above and below. Coyote skin door, and note the tiny bat above the bottom rainbow.

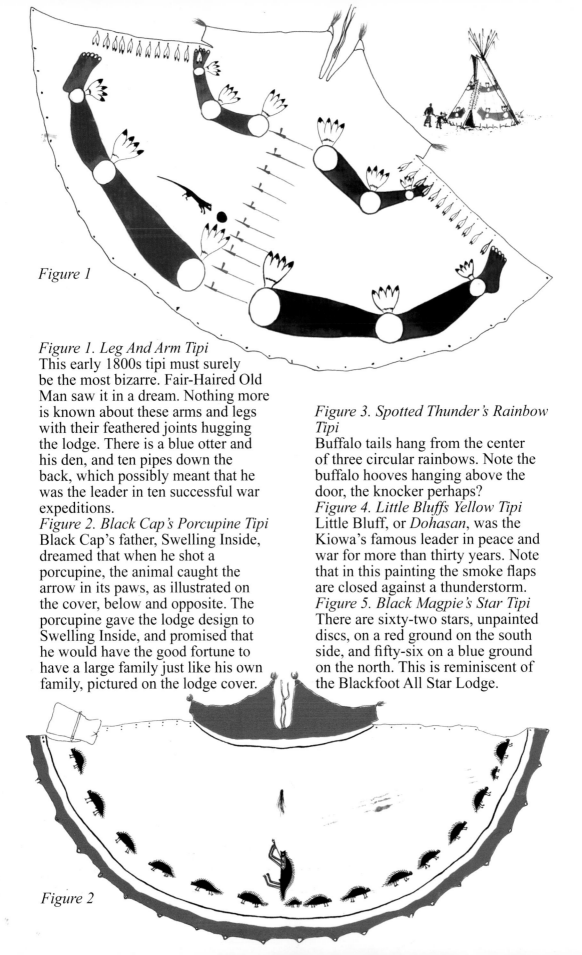

Figure 1. Leg And Arm Tipi

This early 1800s tipi must surely be the most bizarre. Fair-Haired Old Man saw it in a dream. Nothing more is known about these arms and legs with their feathered joints hugging the lodge. There is a blue otter and his den, and ten pipes down the back, which possibly meant that he was the leader in ten successful war expeditions.

Figure 2. Black Cap's Porcupine Tipi

Black Cap's father, Swelling Inside, dreamed that when he shot a porcupine, the animal caught the arrow in its paws, as illustrated on the cover, below and opposite. The porcupine gave the lodge design to Swelling Inside, and promised that he would have the good fortune to have a large family just like his own family, pictured on the lodge cover.

Figure 3. Spotted Thunder's Rainbow Tipi

Buffalo tails hang from the center of three circular rainbows. Note the buffalo hooves hanging above the door, the knocker perhaps?

Figure 4. Little Bluffs Yellow Tipi

Little Bluff, or *Dohasan*, was the Kiowa's famous leader in peace and war for more than thirty years. Note that in this painting the smoke flaps are closed against a thunderstorm.

Figure 5. Black Magpie's Star Tipi

There are sixty-two stars, unpainted discs, on a red ground on the south side, and fifty-six on a blue ground on the north. This is reminiscent of the Blackfoot All Star Lodge.

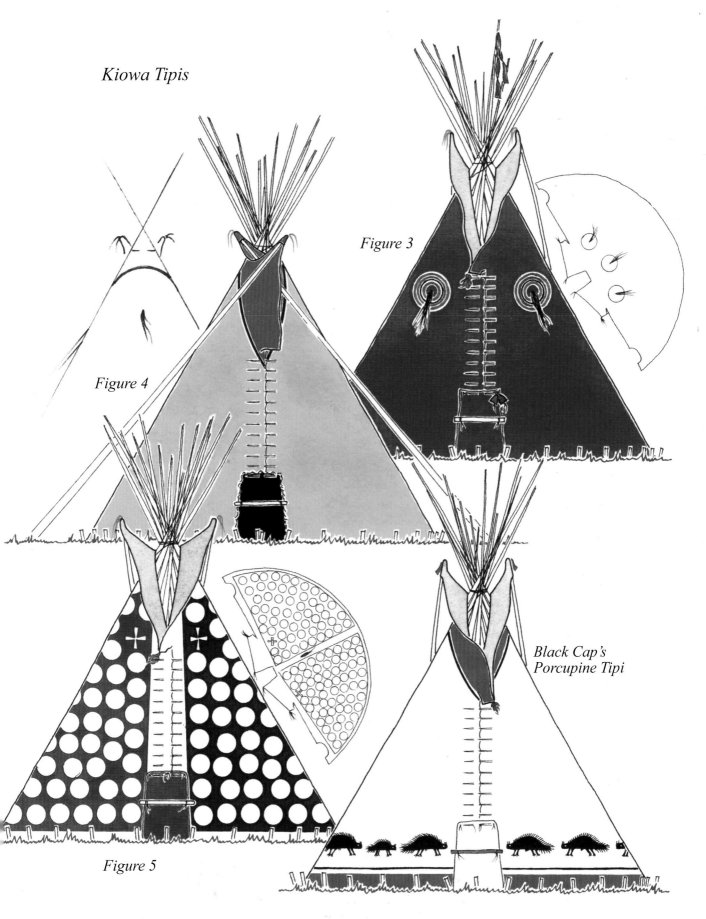

Kiowa Tipis

Figure 3

Figure 4

Figure 5

Black Cap's
Porcupine Tipi

91

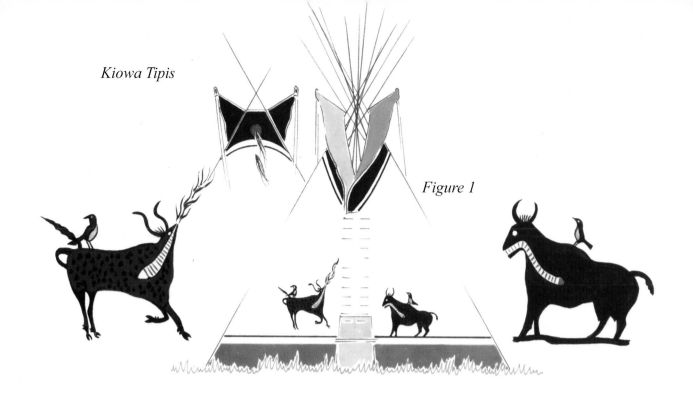

Kiowa Tipis

Figure 1

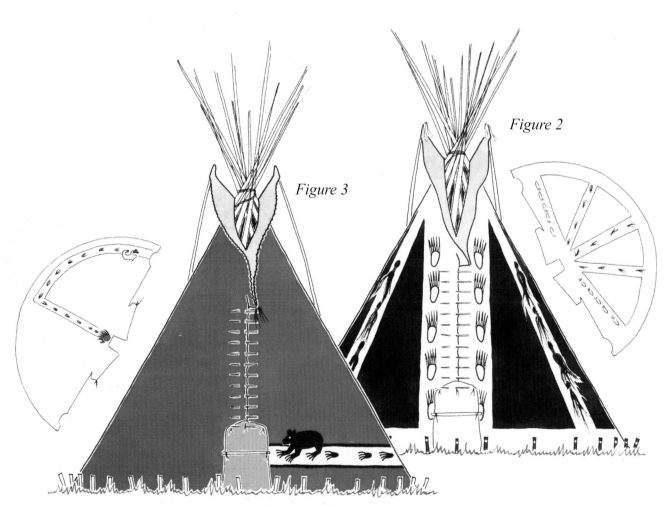

Figure 3

Figure 2

Figure 4

Figure 5

Kiowa Tipis

Figure 1. Blue Top Tipi of Screaming on High
During four days near death with food poisoning, Screaming on High dreamed he saw this lodge with a buffalo on one side of the door, and a long-horn cattle on the other. His vision foresaw that cattle, "spotted buffaloes" (note the blue spots) would replace buffalo. The yellow-breasted birds may be meadowlarks, who give good advice and "talk Indian."

Figure 2. Spotted Thunder's Lodge
With tracks up the front, the bear protects this Kiowa-Apache lodge.

Figure 3. Lodge of Bear Brings It
In this design, the bear has walked down the back of the lodge, along the north side to the door, to protect those within. At the back there is a red leather fringed sun.

Figure 4. Morning Star Tipi
Maltese crosses are the morning star.

Note the rainbows above the "earth" and below the "sky."

Figure 5. Wolf Chief's Ute Lodge
When attacking an Ute village, Wolf Chief struck a painted lodge in front of his fellow warriors, claiming the design as spoils of battle.

Figure 6. Black Ear Tipi
There are blackbirds and yellow-headed blackbirds on the backs of the horses.

Figure 6

93

Tipis From Ledger Book Paintings
The three on the right are Kiowa, all with suns at the back, a feature common with most Kiowa tipis. The red lodge has a striped Navaho blanket for its door. Another has eagle tail fans, a little similar to Big Bow's Tail Tipi (page 85).

The eagle painted lodge is Arapaho, with an adult eagle above and a young eagle below. The tipi was painted by a young man, known only as Henderson, who died aged 23 in 1885. Note the eagle tracks at the top.

Arapaho Lodge (1900)
The tipi at the left belonged to the keeper of the venerated pipe of the Arapaho people. He officiated in a central role at the Sun Dance and all the important ceremonies. The forked red lines are lightning, the yellow discs, suns. The 14 red lines and 13 green, are broken up the back, where there is a crescent moon. As with so many of these lodge designs, we can speculate, but the true meanings of the lines and discs, their numbers and their colors, will never be known.

Two Crow Lodges

These are copied from old (1900s) photographs, the colors speculative. The sacred pipe, or calumet, painted on the above tipi, with its fan of eagle feathers, was recognized by peoples all over North America as the supreme symbol of relationship and peace. It was kept inside a bundle, and cared for by a man and his wife on behalf of the community. Here the bundle is on a tripod behind the tipi. Such bundles were opened with prayers, often at the full or new moon, or at the return of the thunder and life-giving rain in the spring.

Note the guy ropes tied to the lifting pole, and the smoke flap lines. Both of these lodges illustrate the elegant shape and slenderest of poles so loved by Crow people, one set of poles having streamers from the tipis.

The giant eagle on the lodge opposite wraps its protective wings around the lodge, reminiscent of the Kiowa and Blackfoot Hugging Bear Tipis. The eagle flies high among the stars, seeing all things in heaven and earth.

Tipi Sizes Vary

The painting, opposite, illustrates that tipi sizes vary, depending on the number of people who live in them. These Cheyenne lodges vary from a 5-foot child's tipi (measured to where the poles meet), to one 18 feet tall, although tipis may reach as high as 25 feet.

The tallest, which has parallel beadwork stripes and medallions up the back, is called a Blue Stripe Lodge. This is sacred work, done by women, representing great expense of time and skill. Note that the poles are newly cut, with their topmost needles retained. Such thin and fragile tips would not have lasted long during Buffalo Days when poles received rough treatment, dragged from one campsite to another.

The painter illustrates Cheyenne tipis with their characteristically long smoke flaps, yet he paints a Crow Indian gun case hanging from the saddle; a gift, or a battle trophy? Note the Eastern Kingbird atop the tipi pole, a fine perch from which to dart for insects.

The Cheyenne lodge (right) is copied from an old photograph. The "good red earth" as Black Elk called it, seems the right color for the base, and black for the night sky above, with the sun in between.

The pipes down the back indicate that the owner "carried the pipe," or was a successful war party leader, probably raiding the Pawnee or Crow villages for horses, as the many painted horses suggest. Note the traditional movement of the scenes from right to left. The figure paintings are like campaign medals: the owner's brave deeds, pictured for all to see.

The smoke flap poles are crossed, suggesting that the lodge is closed for a cool night, or rain.

At the back, above the bottom border: could those be four enemy scalps?

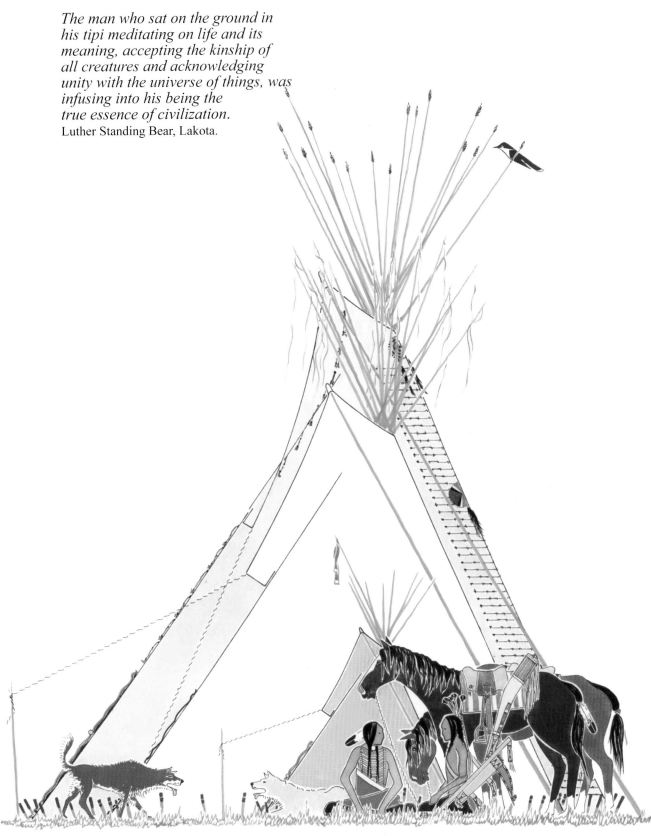

The man who sat on the ground in his tipi meditating on life and its meaning, accepting the kinship of all creatures and acknowledging unity with the universe of things, was infusing into his being the true essence of civilization.
Luther Standing Bear, Lakota.

Tipi Sizes Vary

At Night
Lying down in a tipi thinking about sleep, you feel close to the natural world: you look up at the stars through the smoke hole, while hearing the leaves rustling in the breeze.

"At night when we are about to lie down, listening to the wind rustling through the bleached trees, we do not know how we get to sleep, but we fall asleep."
Crow Indian lullaby.

Perhaps there is an owl hunting, deer browsing, even raindrops on the cover. If there is still the remains of a fire burning, it casts flickering shadows all around, with the occasional creak and crack of embers, until they finally sink down into ashes, and silence.

"In olden days the Indians lived peacefully with all animals. Even the buffalo would often wander into the camp of the Lakotas and eat the grass that grew within the circle of the village. They would usually come during the night, and when the Lakotas awoke in the morning there would be the buffalo. When the smoke began to rise from the tipis and the people began to stir about, the buffalo would move away."
Chief Standing Bear, Lakota.

Cheyenne Tipis
In the above painting, the painter gives the impression that *every* tipi in a Cheyenne camp was painted. A photograph taken in 1880, of a southern Cheyenne camp shows only one painted tipi among more than fifty. However those were the most difficult times for Cheyenne people and tipi painting would have probably been at an all-time low priority.

The above tipis are shown in some detail on the following pages.

Bear Cap's elegant tipi, right, has five rows of buffalo horns, buffalo tails on the smoke flaps, and a lone bull close to the south side of the door. The cover has no door cutouts.

99

the lodge represent the buffalo's closest associates, grasshoppers, in their multitudes and many colors, red, yellow, dark blue, orange, black, and green. They used to say that grasshoppers fly in order to color their wings in the sunlight. Warriors, too, painted diamond shapes on their horses and shields, because in battle they wished for the protection of the grasshoppers' speed and agility.

Whenever hunters could not find the buffalo herds, it was the custom to find a black cricket, and to ask it to point its feelers in the direction they should go to look for the herds. If the cricket pointed one of his feelers backward, there would be a few buffalo in that direction as well. The crickets always knew best.

This Cheyenne lodge belonged to the priest who had charge of the Cheyenne's Sacred Buffalo Hat, *Issiwun*, which took a central place in annual ceremonies to ensure the continuing abundance and welfare of all living things. When the Cheyenne camped in a formal circle, *Issiwun*'s lodge was within the circle toward the south. Also within the circle was the lodge which held the other holy relic, the Sacred Arrows, *Mahuts*.

The painting is copied from an 1889 black-and-white photograph. George Bird Grinnell, who knew the Cheyenne during the early days, may well have seen this very lodge. He wrote: "The hat and arrows lodges were painted black below and red above." The many colored diamond shapes scattered all over

Windbreaks
On the windy plains, tipis were sometimes protected against winter blizzards with windbreaks of cane or willow built upon a framework of posts and poles. This was more common on the southern plains with the southern Cheyenne, Kiowa, and Comanche, although they were used farther north as well. During the early reservation days, when travel was limited, windbreaks were left up year round, also giving privacy and protection from livestock.

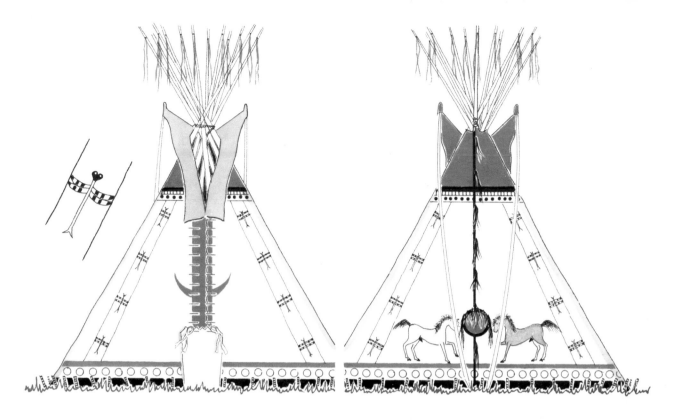

These handsome lodges belonged to a shaman named Glad Road. He was a respected warrior and a berdache, dressing in women's clothing. Shamans did not follow the path of prayer and religion, but were concerned with the occult, whether prophesy, searching for lost objects, calling the buffalo herds, even entertainment or black arts, or, as in Glad Road's case, match-making, love, and sex.

The lodge, right, is copied from an 1860s photograph. Glad Road died in 1879. Above, are the back and front views of a later version of his tipi, made in 1900 as a model for the Smithsonian Institution. This was the lodge upon which Reginald and Gladys Laubin based their painted lodge, authors of the standard work on tipis: *The Indian Tipi—It's History, Construction, and Use*, University of Oklahoma Press, Norman, 1957.

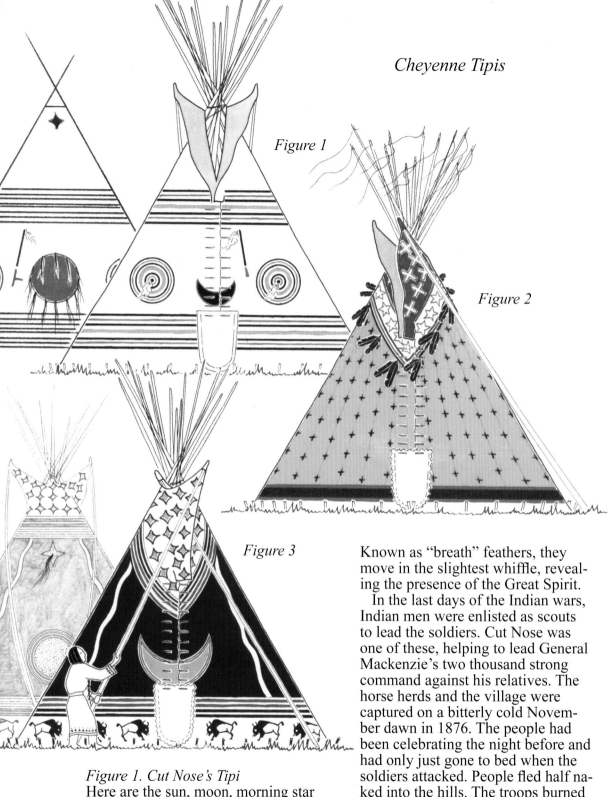

Cheyenne Tipis

Figure 1

Figure 2

Figure 3

Figure 1. Cut Nose's Tipi
Here are the sun, moon, morning star and rainbows. The meaning of the two pipes is not known; one is an archaic straight pipe often used in war, the other a conventional pipe. Eagle breast feathers are attached to the pipe stems and the circular rainbows.

Known as "breath" feathers, they move in the slightest whiffle, revealing the presence of the Great Spirit.

In the last days of the Indian wars, Indian men were enlisted as scouts to lead the soldiers. Cut Nose was one of these, helping to lead General Mackenzie's two thousand strong command against his relatives. The horse herds and the village were captured on a bitterly cold November dawn in 1876. The people had been celebrating the night before and had only just gone to bed when the soldiers attacked. People fled half naked into the hills. The troops burned everything. In terrible cold the people made a harrowing trek to find their Lakota friends, Crazy Horse's people, who gave them shelter.
Figure 2. Mad Bull's Tipi
Figure 3. Red Cloud's Tipi

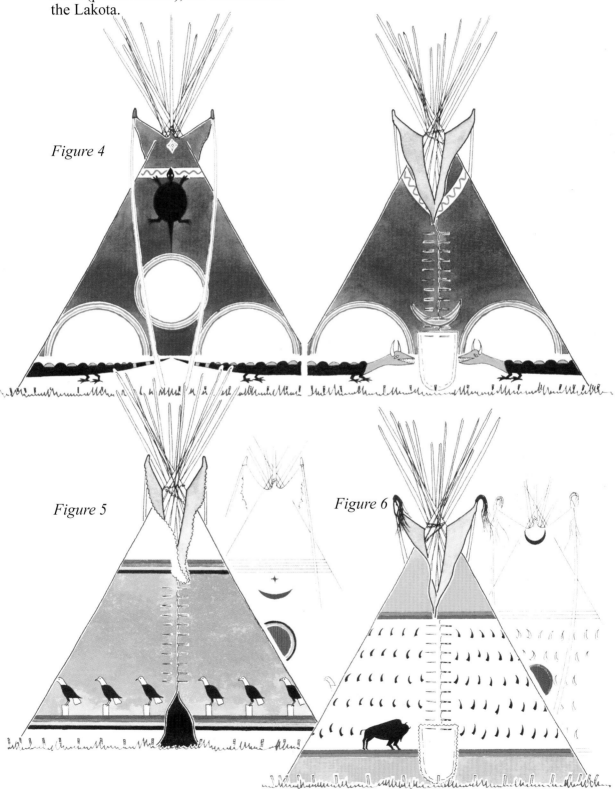

Figure 4. Under-Water Monster Tipi At one time the under-water monsters ruled the earth, they say, but then the thunderbirds conquered them, and they were forced to hide in deep rivers and lakes. This is the *mihn* (plural *mihnio*), the *unktehila* of the Lakota.

Everything here relates to water: turtle, rainbows, the watery sun and moon, and morning star, and the zigzag lightning.
Figure 5. Shining Belly's Tipi
Figure 6. Bear Cap's Tipi

Figure 4

Figure 5

Figure 6

Figure 1. Lame Bull's Tipi
Lame Bull was a healer and war leader. The design of the tipi front is not known because the model is on museum display, showing only the view illustrated. There are probably four blue columns at the semi-cardinal points, joining the sky and earth border. Lame Bull's wife is adjusting the smoke flaps with their buffalo or horse tail finials.

Figure 2. Bull Rib's Tipi

Figure 3. Little Chief's Tipi
This is a half-and-half design of fifteen (*not* fourteen as illustrated) horizontal lines on the south side, with horse tails attached at the back. Note the scalloped smoke flap edges.

Figure 4. Mad Wolf's Tipi
Mad Wolf was one of a few brave Cheyennes and Lakotas who halted Custer's advance into the village at the Little Bighorn river, before the soldiers were driven back up the hill to Custer's "last stand."

Figure 5. Little Rock's Tipi
Jaguars flank the door. In addition to the sun at the back, which is framed with a rainbow, there is a small crescent and disc in pale blue above the door.

Figure 1

Figure 2

Figure 3

Figure 4

Little Rock was killed in late November, 1868, when Custer's cavalry attacked their winter camps along the Washita river. Little Rock had stopped to defend the women and children who were wet and frozen after crossing the river, trying to escape from the soldiers.

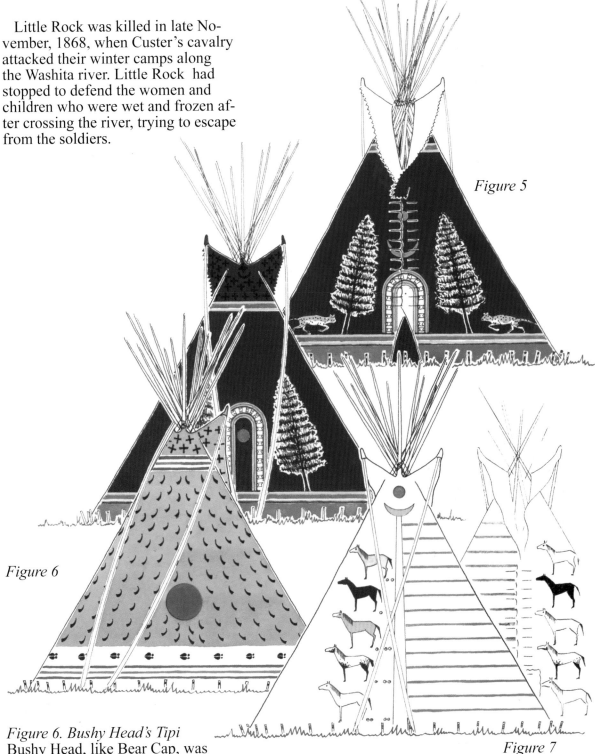

Figure 5

Figure 6

Figure 7

Figure 6. Bushy Head's Tipi
Bushy Head, like Bear Cap, was probably a buffalo caller, both tipis being painted with myriad buffalo horns. Before Indian people had horses, buffalo callers had powers to lure the herds into position so that people could drive them into pounds or over cliffs. Nobody ever knew the buffalo so well.

Figure 7. Starving Coyote's Tipi
This is another half-and-half design, with fourteen horizontal red lines on the south side, and two vertical rows of five horses each. At the top there is a sun and moon, with two lines extending like rays to the base.

The Cheyenne lodges, above left, are painted from a written description. The other lodge is copied from an old photograph. Colors are speculative.

The Cheyenne tipis, below, are taken from ledger book paintings, a rich recourse for tipi designs, although it is never certain which are actual designs, and which invented by the painter. Note the black and white eagle feathers hanging from the smoke flaps.

Ledger Book Painting
Mention has already been made of ledger book paintings: in the old days painting had always been on skins, but when the traders came to Indian Country, they brought pens and pencils, colored pencils and paints. The only paper was the traders' ledger books, and so these early drawings are usually on lined and numbered pages, and are known as ledger book paintings.

Tipi Covers Made with Awning Canvas

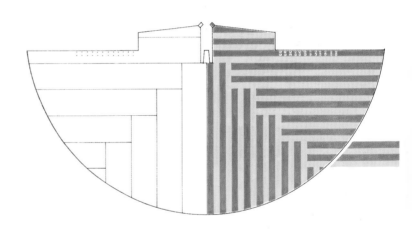

As far back as the 1920s, it was mostly the four-pole peoples of western Montana and Idaho who had a liking for tipi covers made of striped awning canvas. Configurations of plain and striped canvas in different colors and widths gave immense possibilities for variation.

In the 1950s, the red and yellow striped tipi, above, belonged to Alba and Hattie Shawaway, traditional leaders of their three-pole Yakima people. They adopted the painter of these pages and gave him the name, *In-chee yow-ail-look-sha-why-ama*, (Alba's spelling), Great Rising Eagle.

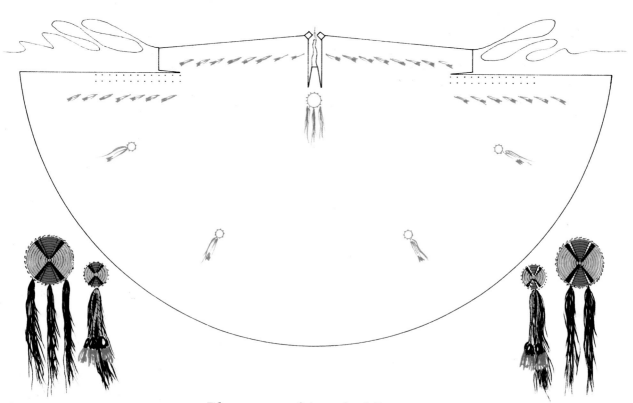

Placement of Attached Designs
Cheyenne and Arapaho Blue Stripe and White Stripe Tipi designs:
large Sun medallion, four Four Winds roundels, and thirty pendants.

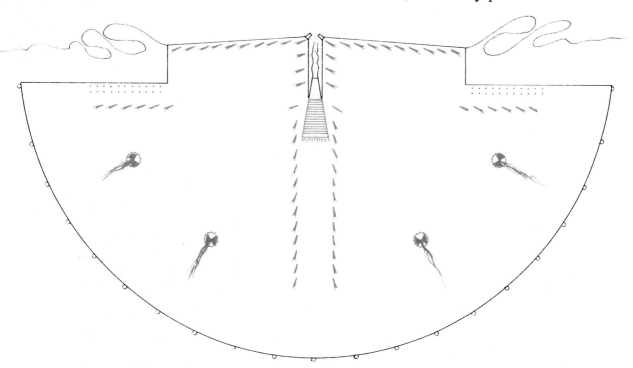

Placement of Lakota Attached Designs
Large trapezoid Sun, four Four Winds roundels, and multiple pendants.

Tipis with Attached Decorations

In a tipi village there were only a few painted tipis, but a number would have had attached decorations in the form of colored discs and pendants. Formerly embroidered with dyed porcupine quills, today they are mostly beadwork, but some women are reluctant to use these beautiful attachments because unscrupulous tourists unpick them.

The tradition of attachments may have originated with the Cheyenne and Arapaho, with the Lakota and other peoples imitating and adding their own ideas. The Arapaho and Cheyenne have many named designs, each with a specific intent: Ghost Tipi for burials, Family Tipis, a Chief's Tipi, a Newlyweds Tipi, given by a mother-in-law to honor her son-in-law. There are designs known as the Thunderbird Tipi, Star Tipi, White Stripe and Blue Stripe Tipis, and the Striped Tipi which is illustrated on page 97.

Each design has a large medallion sewn to the cover at the back just below the tie tongue; this is called the Sun. There are four smaller roundels sewn to the cover at the semi-cardinal points, marking the Four Winds. In addition there are eight pendants attached to each smoke flap, close to where the flap joins the cover, and seven pendants either side of the lacing pins, making a total of thirty.

All these attachments are often referred to as "tipi ornaments" or "decorations," but the words suggest something slightly frivolous, whereas they mark the heavens and the four directions, thus fixing the sacred center of each home amidst the surrounding enormity of the Great Plains. Pendants and horse hair tassels rustle in the breeze and in a high wind the dew-claws which hang below the four roundels, drum against the cover. All of these beautiful things have an ancient and mysterious lineage, and only a few are illustrated here. (For more details see *References:* Coleman and Kroeber.)

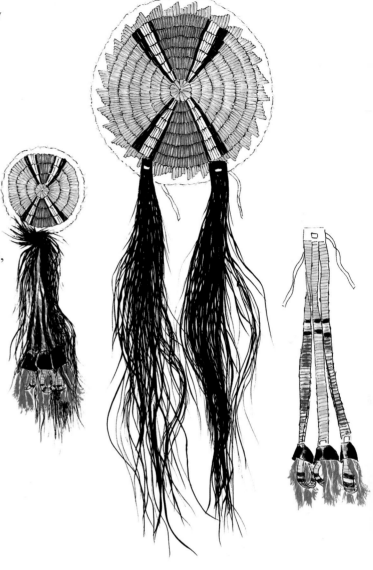

Designs for White Stripe Tipi

The Sun disc, about eight inches diameter, has two hanks of horsehair, formerly buffalo beard, sewn to the bottom edge.

The Four Winds roundels, about four inches diameter, are sewn to the cover a little above door height. Each has tassels sewn to the bottom edge, consisting of a hank of horsehair, three buckskin thongs and loops wrapped with cornhusk, dew-claws, and wool tufts.

Each tipi has about thirty pendants.

109

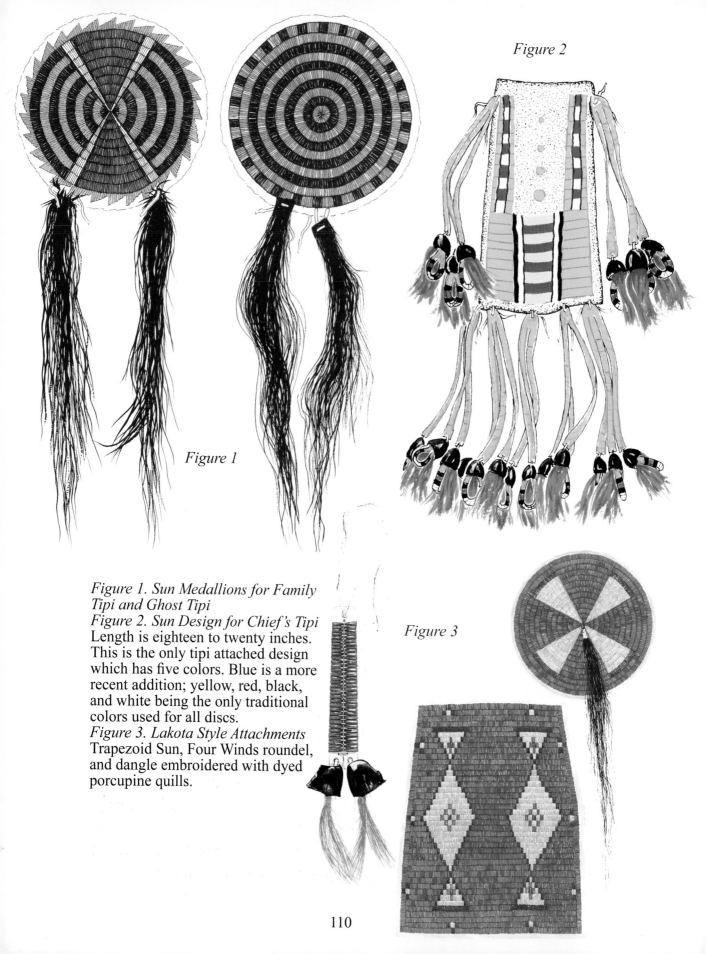

Figure 1

Figure 2

Figure 3

Figure 1. Sun Medallions for Family Tipi and Ghost Tipi

Figure 2. Sun Design for Chief's Tipi
Length is eighteen to twenty inches. This is the only tipi attached design which has five colors. Blue is a more recent addition; yellow, red, black, and white being the only traditional colors used for all discs.

Figure 3. Lakota Style Attachments
Trapezoid Sun, Four Winds roundel, and dangle embroidered with dyed porcupine quills.

Tipi Rings

Should you come across a rough ring of stones in the grass, it could be a "tipi ring," the spot where stones were pushed away from the floor of the tipi, and used instead of pegs to hold down the cover around the bottom. It would have been a winter camp, perhaps a burial lodge. Look for the entrance at the east, for all tipis face the sun's first rays. Sit down at the west, looking out of the *door*, and meditate on the feeling of the place. The *fireplace* is right in front of you; *men* sitting at your left, *women* to your right. They are glad you have come. Food and water is placed in front of you.

Over the thousands of years Indian peoples lived and hunted on the Plains, they left very few marks on the land: the occasional tipi ring, indication of a fireplace, scattered pieces of shell, or flint where they chipped arrowheads, small piles of stones leading to a buffalo pound, an overgrown hilltop pit where they caught eagles; nothing more.

When a Tipi Cover was Worn Out

Buffalo hide tipi covers lasted from three to five years, the bottom tearing and rotting first. This could be trimmed, but it left a smaller interior. This was sometimes given away to poorer people, but even if the cover was to be replaced, the best parts were put to a number of uses: tipi linings, leggings, moccasins and more, because this was tanned leather, well smoked and used, soft and waterproof.

When a sacred painted cover was replaced, the old cover was returned to the spirits who had given it. Blackfoot people sometimes took an old cover to a lake among the mountains where it was sunk with rocks, a gift to the water spirits. Usually covers were staked to the ground in a remote place, an offering to the Sun. Here, in the rather topsy-turvy painting opposite, the cover of a Blackfoot Crow Lodge has been left with the winds and rain, the prairie dogs and the flowers. Each takes a part as it returns to Mother Earth.

Burial Lodge

Sometimes when a person died, the body was left inside the tipi, clothed in its finest, wrapped in buffalo robes, and laid on a bed. The smoke hole and door were tied shut, and rocks weighted down the cover around the bottom to keep out animals, and then the people moved away, leaving the deceased to travel the Spirit Trail (Milky Way) to the Land of Many Tipis. The close family members lived with relatives for a period of mourning. Meanwhile the burial tipi remained undisturbed for as long as it withstood the elements, except when white people came and stripped the contents for souvenirs.

In the above painting, the painter has pictured the tipi in a sheltered fold of the ground, within sight of the Great Spirit's holy hill, Bear Butte, place of pilgrimage for many peoples through the ages, including Cheyenne, Lakota, Mandan, and Arikara.

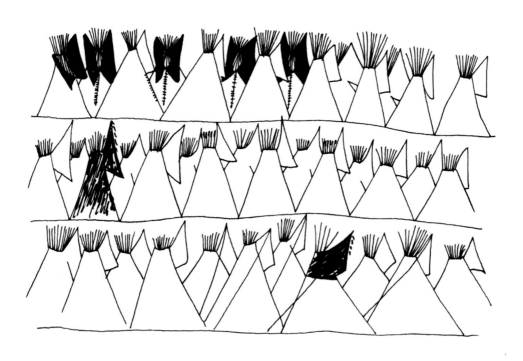

Postscript

Most of the tipis in this book are history, and the texts generally speak of times past: in the beginning ... in the old days ... during Buffalo Days ... at one time there was ... it used to be ...

But the tradition continues: this striking Beaver Lodge was recently added to the inner circle of Blackfoot lodges, at the Browning Indian Days in northwestern Montana.

References

Brasser, Ted J., *Pedigree of Hugging Bear Tipi,* American Indian Art Magazine, Vol 5, No 1, 1979.

Campbell, Stanley, *The Cheyenne Tipi*, American Anthropologist, Vol 17, No 4, New York, 1915.

———. *The Tipis of the Crow Indians*, American Anthropologist, Vol 29, No 1, New York, 1927.

Coleman, Winfield W., *The Cheyenne Women's Sewing Society in Design Symbology and Decoration*, Buffalo Bill Historical Center, Cody, 1980.

Denver Art Museum, *The Plains Indian Tipi*, Leaflet No 19, 1931.

Ewers, John C., *Murals in the Round - Painted Tipis of the Kiowa and Kiowa--Apache Indians*, Smithsonian Institution, Washington, 1978.

Fagin, Nancy I., *The James Mooney Collection of Cheyenne Tipi Models at the Field Museum of Natural History*, Plains Anthropologist, 1988.

Grinnell, George Bird, *The Lodges of the Blackfeet*, American Anthropologist, Vol 3, New York, 1901.

Indian Arts and Crafts Board, US Dept of the Interior, *Painted Tipis by Contemporary Plains Indian Artists*, Anadarko, Oklahoma, 1973.

Laubin, Reginald and Gladys, *The Indian Tipi - Its History, Construction, and Use*, University of Oklahoma Press, Norman, 1957.

Kroeber. Alfred L., *The Arapaho*, University of Nebraska Press, Lincoln, 1983.

McClintock, Walter, *The Old North Trail - Life, Legends and Religion of the Blackfeet Indians*, Macmillan, London, 1910.

———. *Painted Tipis and Picture Writing of the Blackfeet Indians*, Leaflet No 6, Southwest Museum, Los Angeles.

——— . *The Blackfoot Tipi*, Leaflet No 5, Southwest Museum, Los Angeles.

Museum of the Rockies, *Tipis - Design and Legend*, Bozeman, Montana, 1976.

Nabakov, Peter and Robert Easton, *Native American Architecture*, Oxford University, New York, 1989.

Nomadics Tipi Makers*, Instructions for Setting up a Sioux Tipi*, Bend, Oregon.

Thybony, Scott, *The Tipi - Portable Home of the Plains*, Western National Parks Association, 2003.

Yue, David and Charlotte, *The Indian Tipi - A Center of Native American Life*, Knopf, New York, 1984.

Index